KU-470-258

BANTAM BOOKS

TORONTO • NEW YORK • LONDON • SYDNEY • AUCKLAND

MARINES
by
Edwin H. Simmons

FLOWERS ON THE BEACH

The 9th Marine Expeditionary Brigade, the first combat troops into Vietnam, land at Da Nang on March 8, 1965. As the Marines charged on to Red Beach 2, carrying 80 lb packs, the only obstacles they encountered were smiling college girls.

CHASING CHARLIE

Hotel Company, 2d Battalion, 5th Marines heading into the hills south of Da Nang on a search-and-destroy mission.

DEFENDING THE DMZ
CH-46 Sea Knights create
an instant landing zone as
the 1st Battalion, 4th
Marines deploy south of
the 17th Parallel near
Khe Sanh.

EDITORS: Richard Ballantine, Richard Grant. PHOTO RESEARCH: John Moore.
DRAWINGS: John Batchelor. MAPS: Peter Williams. STUDIO: Kim Williams.
PRODUCED BY: The Up & Coming Publishing Company, Bearsville, New York.

MARINES
THE ILLUSTRATED HISTORY OF THE VIETNAM WAR
A Bantam Book/ August 1987

ACKNOWLEDGEMENTS

*The writer wishes to thank the staff of the Marine Corps Historical Center
and others who contributed to this book. I wish to thank particularly official
historians Mr Jack Shulimson; Dr V. Keith Fleming,Jr;
Mr Charles R. Smith, and Major G. Ross Dunham,USMC,
for their careful reading of the manuscript.
Further, I should like to thank Mr Danny J. Crawford and the members of
his Reference Section, especially for verifying the information on Medal of
Honor recipients; Mrs Regina Strother for assistance in locating photographs;
and Miss Evelyn A. Englander, the librarian for her unfailing aid in finding
secondary sources.*

*Photographs for this book were selected from the archives of DAVA, the
USMC and Military Archive Research Services*

All rights reserved
Copyright © 1987 Rufus Publications, Inc
*This book may not be reproduced in whole or in part, by mimeograph or
any other means, without permission.
For information address: Bantam Books, Inc*

Library of Congress Cataloging-in-Publication Data

Simmons, Edwin H., 1921-
Marines.

1. Vietnamese Conflict, 1961-1975—United States.
2. United States. Marine Corps—History—Vietnamese
Conflict, 1961-1975. I. Title.
DS558.S53   1987   959.704′342   86-47565
ISBN 0-553-34448-X

Published simultaneously in the United States and Canada

*Bantam Books are published by Bantam Books, Inc. Its trademark, consisting of the
words "Bantam Books" and the portrayal of a rooster, is Registered in U.S. Patent
and Trademark Office and in other countries. Marca Registrada. Bantam Books, Inc.,
666 Fifth Avenue, New York, New York 10103.*

PRINTED IN THE UNITED STATES OF AMERICA

CW   0   9   8   7   6   5   4   3   2

Contents

Flowers on the Beach

First in . .

THE 9th Marine Expeditionary Brigade received its orders about noon local time, 7 March 1965. Navy Task Force 76 carrying the Marines was five or six hours from the Bay of Da Nang, wallowing up and down in foul weather.

Slim, dapper Brigadier General Frederick J. Karch, its commander, helicoptered ashore to work out the details with Vietnamese I Corps and the US staff officers up from Military Advisory Command, Vietnam, in Saigon. H-Hour was 0800 the next morning.

By that time the rain had slackened and the wind was down to a reasonable eight knots. But there were still eight-to-ten-foot swells out in the transport area so L-Hour was delayed until 0900. The Marines landed on Red Beach, a sandy crescent just west of the city and a mile or so north of the runway of the Da Nang air base. The first wave of Battalion Landing Team 3/9 touched down at 0902. "They came ashore," General Westmoreland later wrote, "in full battle regalia as if re-enacting Iwo Jima . . ."

But to the embarrassment of the Marines, the war was not on Red Beach. As they disembarked from amphibian tractors, each hunched down under 60-80 pounds of combat gear, they were confronted by girls with arms filled with flowers, very pretty girls with long straight black hair and flowing white silk *ao dais* over black silk trousers.

The beaming Mayor of Da Nang had arranged this welcome. A photograph of an unsmiling thin-mustached General Karch, garlanded in flowers, went off to the world via Associated Press.

Also present was General Nguyen Chanh Thi, commanding general of the I Corps, in his favorite uniform—the red beret and the mottled purple and

US ambassador Maxwell Taylor —questioned the introduction of US ground combat forces.

Gen. William C. Westmoreland —as Commander, US Military Advisory Command, Vietnam, commanded US combat forces in the country until 1968. He criticized the Marines' defensive capabilities.

green camouflage suit of the Airborne Brigade. Four hundred miles to the south in Saigon, Ambassador Maxwell Taylor was not amused by the spectacle on Red Beach. He had words with General William C. Westmoreland, COMUSMACV, standing stiffly at attention in front of him.

A month earlier, Westmoreland had sent his deputy, Lieutenant General John L. Throckmorton, north to Da Nang. Throckmorton recommended that the 9th MEB be landed to solidify the defense of the air base. Westmoreland's message requesting the landing went forward on Washington's birthday, 22 February. Ambassador Taylor had dispatched a cable to the State Department giving his reluctant concurrence. Questioning the usefulness of US ground troops, he said in clipped cablese: "White faced soldier armed, equipped and trained as he is not suitable guerrilla fighter for Asian forests and jungles. French tried to adapt their forces to this mission and failed; I doubt US forces could do much better. Furthermore, we would have vastly complicating factor of not running war and hence problem of arranging satisfactory command relationships with our Vietnamese allies."

In Honolulu, Westmoreland's immediate superior, Admiral Ulysses S. Grant Sharp, Commander-in-Chief, Pacific, disagreed. In a message that owed something to the facile pen of the Commanding General, Fleet Marine Force, Pacific, Lieutenant General Victor H. Krulak, Sharp opined that the Marines could provide "a tight defense of the airfield complex and good security of US outlying installations." As for Taylor's gloomy prediction concerning the effectiveness of "white faced" soldiers, Sharp snorted, "This stands athwart past performance in this function. The Marines have a distinguished record in counter-guerrilla warfare."

The Joint Chiefs added their favorable endorsement and Westmoreland's request went to Secretary of Defense Robert S. McNamara, who took it to President Lyndon B. Johnson. On 26 February, the State Department directed Taylor to seek South Vietnamese approval for the landing. This he got, but with the caveat that the Marines be landed "in the most inconspicuous way feasible."

Somehow the distinction between 'battalion' and 'battalion landing team' escaped the old paratroop

eneral. What he understood would be a light infan-
ry force turned out to be a thundering procession
f Marines coming ashore with a full panoply of
anks and artillery, including a pair of nuclear-
apable 8-inch guns.

Karch's second battalion landing team, BLT 1/3,
vas more lightly configured and came in from
)kinawa in Marine Corps KC-130 Hercules
ransports. The first aircraft landed at 1100, its ap-
roach over the rice paddies south of Da Nang draw-
ng a patter of Viet Cong rifle fire.

The arriving Marines interfered with the regular
ommercial air traffic and with still a third of 1st
3attalion, 3d Marines, to land, the airlift was halted.
The Marines broke out shelter halves and camped
round the airfield while their disposition was be-
ng decided. Two days passed before all of BLT 1/3
vas brought in.

The 1st Battalion, 3d Marines, stayed on the air-
ield to provide perimeter defense. The 3d Battalion,
)th Marines, moved up onto Hill 327 just west of the
air base. Marines would be on Hill 327 (327 meters,
r about 1,073 feet, above sea level) for the next six
years on what would come to be called 'Division
Ridge.'

Battalions were the chess pieces of the Vietnam

**Adm. Ulysses
S. Grant Sharp
—countered
Ambassador
Taylor's
doom-laden
predictions.**

STRAIGHT IN:
**As soon as
they landed
Marines from
BLT 1/3 were
deployed to
defend the
perimeter of
Da Nang
air base.
The KC-130F
transport-
refueler was
the Marine
version of the
Lockheed
C-130 Hercules.
It could lift 92
combat-
equipped
troops or re-
fuel two jet
aircraft.**

15

TOUCH & GO:
Under enemy
fire Vietnamese
troops and US
advisors
unload a
helicopter in a
fast-action re-
supply
operation.
S.Vietnam
established its
own Marine
Corps in 1954
at the
instigation of a
US Marine
officer, Col.
Victor J.
Croizat, USMC.
The
Vietnamese
Marines
regularly sent
officers for
training at the
USMC school
at Quantico.

**S.Vietnam's
three
jet-capable
airfields**

War—to be moved about the chessboard by division and corps commanders and often by Washington, Honolulu, and Saigon.

Westmoreland was impressed that Marine battalions were heavy in infantry, with four rifle companies of over 200 men each. This gave them staying power, valuable so close to the North Vietnamese border. Later he delivered a more crabbed judgment: "I had not realized at the time that Marines were poorly trained in defensive warfare and were reluctant to dig in sufficiently for long defensive engagements . . ."

Da Nang air base was the northernmost of South Vietnam's three jet-capable fields, the others being Ton Son Nhut and Bien Hoa, close to Saigon. The new 10,000-foot concrete runway ran almost due north and south. Even before the arrival of Karch's brigade, there were 1,300 Marines at Da Nang. US Marine helicopters had been operating there since 1962. The Marine helicopter squadrons were on the west side of the field, billeted in crumbling old one-story French barracks, mixed in with bits and pieces of Vietnamese units. A Marine Corps light anti-aircraft missile battalion, with Hawk missiles, had arrived in February.

On the east side of the field were Vietnamese Air Force and US Air Force flight operations.For nearly a year the US Air Force had been flying F-100s, F-102s, F-105s, and B-57s from Da Nang. Also there was the terminal for Air Vietnam and other commercial flights. Behind the shops and hangars was military dependents' housing. A ring of old concrete blockhouses linked with belts of rusting barbed wire marked ominously with triangles of tin signifying minefields circled the field. Outside the wire on the west was what the Americans called 'Dog Patch,' a collection of bars, laundries, tailor shops, and less savory enterprises.

Within mortar range lived some quarter-million Vietnamese of various political persuasions. Intelligence credited the Viet Cong with 12 battalions—6,000 men—within striking distance, more than enough to overrun the field's indifferent defenses.

General Thi's I Corps headquarters were in a handsome French-built quadrangle just east of the airfield, its galleried two-story buildings freshly painted ochre with reddish-brown trim. Two chains of command extended down from Thi, one political and one military. The political chain ran through the province chiefs to the district chiefs, then all Vietnamese Army officers.

There were about 10,000 square miles in I Corps' Tactical Zone, 225 miles from north to south, as narrow as 30 miles and at no point wider than 70. I Corps' northern boundary was the Demilitarized Zone, the frontier with North Vietnam. Usually given as the 17th Parallel the line, as defined at Geneva, was actually a river, the Song Ben Hai, as far west as the hamlet of Bo Ho Su. From there it ran in a straight line through the forested hills to the Laotian border.

The northern two provinces, Quang Tri and Thua Thien, were separated from Quang Nam province by the Hai Van mountains, a spur out of the Annamite chain. These mountains drop precipitously to the water's edge, forming the northern arm of the Bay of Da Nang. In March 1965 it was possible to go to the Imperial City of Hue, 50 miles

**I Corps Tactical Zone, the northernmost of S.Vietnam's four tactical zones.
ICTZ covered 10,000 square miles and stretched 225 miles from north to south.**

Flowers on the Beach

GOING IN: Armed with an M-60 machine gun, the door gunner of the UH-34 helicopter keeps watch as Marines of Battalion Landing Team 3/4 (3d Battalion, 4th Marines) get their first taste of Vietnam on the shuttle north from Da Nang to Phu Bai near Hue.

Flowers on the Beach

SAFE LANDINGS:
The Marines made scores of landings along the coast of ICTZ, either to begin an operation or reinforce an action. Unlike the contested beachheads of World War II these landings seldom ran into resistance. Viet Cong guerrilla warfare tactics avoided head-on confrontations and relied on drawing US forces into situations where they could not use their weapons superiority to advantage.

to the north, by the Trans-Vietnam Railway, the line crossing the Nam O bridge and going past the Esso terminal at Lieu Chau before burrowing through many tunnels. Highway One, the old Mandarin Road, roughly paralleled the railroad.

Quang Nam was similarly set off from the two southern provinces by the Que Sons, another mountain spur running from the Annamites almost to the sea (and not to be confused with the Khe Sanh battle area). I Corps' southern boundary, separating

Quang Ngai province from Binh Dinh, was another spur from the Annamites coming down to the sea near Sa Huynh. This division of Thi's domain into three distinct geographic compartments would greatly influence future operations.

Thi commanded on paper a strength of 60,000 men—25,000 'ARVN,' or regular Army of Vietnam, 12,000 'RFs,' or Regional Force provincial troops, and 23,000 'PFs,' or Popular Force district militia—but this impressive total was spread thin over five

The Vietnamese Marines' emblem was almost identical to that of the USMC. The insignia retained the elements of eagle, anchor and globe but where the USMC badge depicts the Americas, the Vietnamese superimposed a star and map of Vietnam.

provinces. Quang Tri and Thua Thien were garrisoned by the ARVN 1st Division, reputedly South Vietnam's best. The southern two provinces, Quang Tin and Quang Ngai, were the fiefdom of the ARVN 2d Division. The center province of Quang Nam was a special sector garrisoned by the ARVN 51st Regiment. This all diagrammed very nicely, but readily available for maneuver Thi had only two or three lightweight Ranger battalions and sometimes a battalion or so of Vietnamese Marines or Airborne troops on assignment from Saigon.

A further complication, was that General Thi did not really command the airfield. Its operation and defense rested with the Vietnamese Air Force, whose senior officer present, a lieutenant colonel, reported directly to Air Vice Marshal Nguyen Cao Ky. An eventual showdown between Thi and Ky was inevitable, with one observer describing Thi as a tiger and Ky as a leopard, the tiger being more violent, the leopard more supple.

A squadron of Marine F-4s arrived at Da Nang on 10 April. Next day, a Marine battalion landing team came ashore. Three days later another battalion landing team from Okinawa, was flown to Phu Bai, an airstrip near Hue, and, more importantly, the base facility for the U. S. Army's 8th Radio Research unit—'research' being the interception and decoding of enemy radio traffic.

On 20 April Taylor and Westmoreland went to a conference called by McNamara at Sharp's CinCPac headquarters in Honolulu. McNamara made it clear that the main war effort would be in the South, not air strikes against the North. The agreed strategy was to break the will of the North Vietnamese and Viet Cong by denying them victory. More ground forces would be needed.

President Johnson approved the landing of the 3d Marine Expeditionary Brigade south of Da Nang and the deployment of the 173d Airborne Brigade to Bien Hoa. Taylor, in discussing the deployments with Dr Phat Huy Quat, South Vietnam's new premier, did not think the time was right to bring up combined command arrangements.

Major General William R. 'Rip' Collins, Commanding General, 3d Marine Division, arrived at Da Nang on 3 May. Three days later Karch's 9th MEB was deactivated and absorbed into the III Marine

Expeditionary Force under Collins. Ground elements were consolidated under the 3d Marine Regiment and aviation elements under Marine Aircraft Group 16.

Some sensitive soul in Saigon had pointed out that the Marines' use of 'Expeditionary' might remind the Vietnamese of the bad old French days. Westmoreland asked for a less emotion-laden descriptor and next day 'III Marine *Expeditionary* Force' became 'III Marine *Amphibious* Force'—almost always contracted to 'III MAF.'

On 7 May the 3d Marine Expeditionary Brigade landed unopposed 57 miles southeast of Da Nang. Like all Marine brigades, 3d MAB was an air-ground task force. It brought ashore the 4th Marine Regiment and a supporting helicopter squadron.

Brig. Gen. Marion E. Carl —commanded 3d MEB.

The beachhead reminded Marines who had served at Camp Lejeune or Cherry Point of North Carolina's broad sandy beaches and pine barrens—and mosquitoes and flies. There was no name on the map so Krulak supplied 'Chu Lai', his name rendered in Mandarin Chinese.

At Honolulu, Krulak had recommended that a Marine expeditionary airfield, 'SATS' for Short Airfield for Tactical Support, be installed at Chu Lai. As developed by the Marines it was a kind of aircraft carrier deck ashore. McNamara asked how long it would take. Krulak said 25 days, compared to 11 months for a concrete runway.

The commander of the 3d Marine Expeditionary Brigade was Brigadier General Marion E. Carl, a leading Marine Corps ace in World War II (18½ kills), a pioneer in both helicopters and jets, and an aeronautical engineer.

Lt. Gen. Victor H. Krulak —nicknamed 'The Brute' because of his diminutive size. He lent his real name to an unmarked beach used by the Marines 57 miles south of Da Nang. Translated into Mandarin Chinese Krulak became 'Chu Lai.'

The day after the Chu Lai landing, Westmoreland sent the JCS a three-stage concept of operations for U. S. and third-country forces. Stage I would be the security of base areas with patrolling limited to light artillery range. Stage II would be deep patrolling and offensive operations outside assigned tactical areas of responsibility. Stage III would be long-range search-and-destroy and reserve reaction operations.

Westmoreland also foresaw four phases of operations. Phase I, securing coastal enclaves; Phase II, operations against the enemy from coastal bases; Phase III, movement inland to secure additional bases; Phase IV, operations from inland bases. For

Flowers on the Beach

SMILES & FLOWERS: The rare flicker of a smile crosses the face of landing force commander Brig. Gen. Frederick Karch. The normally stern Karch disapproved of the whole exercise. On a previous visit he denounced Vietnam as a 'cancer' and suggested the Marines would be better deployed invading N.Vietnam. Gen. Nguyen Chanh Thi (right) who provided the floral welcome, commanded ICTZ. Within a year he was deposed and exiled to the USA with a generous allowance.

the moment the Marines in I Corps were in Phase I, Stage I. Taylor, who found it hard to remember that he was an ambassador and no longer Chairman of the Joint Chiefs of Staff, wryly noted that the greatest threat to the Marines at Da Nang and the 173d Airborne Brigade at Bien Hoa, confined as they were to their bases, was boredom.

General Wallace M. Greene, Jr., the Marine Corps' Commandant, flew in from Washington in late April and, impatient with what he considered half-measures, told the press that his Marines were not in Vietnam "to sit on their ditty boxes" but "to kill

Viet Cong". Meanwhile, the Marines were suffering casualties, nearly two hundred by the first of June, including 18 killed.

The chains of command from Vietnam to Washington were a delicate and zealously guarded balance of operational requirements and service prerogatives. Westmoreland's Military Assistance Command, Vietnam, was a subordinate unified command under Sharp's Pacific Command. Westmoreland, as COMUSMACV, had operational command of all 'in-country' US forces, including the 2d Air Division and III Marine Amphibious Force,

Gen. Wallace M. Greene, Jr. —Marine Corps commandant who wanted his men to take the fight to the enemy.

McDonnell Douglas A-4E Skyhawk: single-seat attack bomber armed with two 20mm cannon and capable of carrying 8,500 lb. payload. Used chiefly for close-air support.

but this operational command did not extend beyond the boundaries of South Vietnam.

Pacific Command had three service 'components': US Army, Pacific; Pacific Air Force, and Pacific Fleet. Each component provided forces to Military Assistance Command, Vietnam. Westmoreland was also Commanding General, US Army, Vietnam. Lieutenant General Joseph H. Moore, USAF, commanded the Air Force 'component' of MACV, the 2d Air Division (later to become the Seventh Air Force). Command functions, other than control of operations, flowed through component channels.

III MAF was administratively subordinate to Krulak's Fleet Marine Force, Pacific. FMFPac was technically part of the Pacific Fleet, but under Krulak's aggressive generalship, FMFPac tended to function as a fourth service component directly under Pacific Command, a practice enhanced by the location of Krulak's headquarters in the same one-time World War II hospital building at Camp H. M. Smith on Oahu as Sharp's headquarters.

On 11 May Major General Paul J. Fontana arrived at Da Nang and opened the forward headquarters of the 1st Marine Aircraft Wing, the 3d Marine Division's aviation counterpart. Both Collins and Fontana were at the end of their year-long Western Pacific tours. General Greene, with very definite ideas on how to fight the war, chose replacements with great care. For the 1st Marine Aircraft Wing he picked Brigadier General Keith B. McCutcheon, the Marine Corps' top aviation theoretician and planner. The slight, taciturn McCutcheon, as operations officer of the Marine aircraft group supporting MacArthur in the Philippines, had systematized close air support, winning medals and high praise from the Army.

After the war, with a master's degree in aeronautical engineering from Massachusetts Institute of Technology, he pioneered the use of jet engines in military aircraft. Later he commanded the Marine Corps' experimental helicopter squadron at Quantico, which led to command of the first transport helicopter squadron in combat in Korea. His last assignment before Vietnam was as the J-3, or operations, officer of the Pacific Command.

By Memorial Day 4,000 feet of aluminum planks had been laid at Chu Lai. On 1 June, the first

CHANGING INDOORS:
Gen. Greene's choice for commander Maj. Gen. Lewis W. Walt (left) strides through the Officers Mess at Da Nang after taking command of III MAF from Maj. Gen. William R. Collins (right). The ceremony took place indoors as the rules of engagement forbade the display of US colors outdoors.

Marine A-4 Skyhawks flew in from the Philippines. The catapult launchers needed to complete the system had not arrived, but the Marine attack planes got off with the extra boost of JATO (jet-assist take-off) bottles.

For the dual command of the 3d Marine Division and the III Marine Amphibious Force Greene went down the list of Marine Corps major generals until he came to the newly-promoted Lewis W. Walt.

Few Marines had combat records to match Walt's. It went back to the defense of the International Settlement in Shanghai in 1937 with the 4th Marines in company with then-Captain Wally Greene. Walt had commanded a company of Edson's Raiders at Tulagi in August 1942. Promoted to major he was given the 2d Battalion, 5th Marines, in time for the hard October and November fighting on Guadalcanal, during which he was wounded, awarded a Silver Star, and field promoted to lieutenant colonel. Later, after landing at Cape Gloucester in

Brig. Gen. Keith B. McCutcheon —top aviation theoretician chosen by Greene to command the 1st Marine Aircraft Wing.

December 1943, he was switched to command the
3d Battalion and in the fight for Aogiri Ridge put
his shoulder to a 37mm gun and blasted his way to
the top. Aogiri Ridge became Walt's Ridge and Walt
received a Navy Cross. At Peleliu in September
1944, again commanding the 3d Battalion, 5th
Marines, he held off a Japanese counterattack at the
airfield and received his second Navy Cross.

In Korea, as a colonel, he commanded the 5th Marines, one of the oldest of Marine Corps regiments,

and in February and March 1953 fought the bitter battles for the outposts Carson, Reno, and Vegas.

For the three years before coming to Vietnam Walt was the Director of the Landing Force Development Center at Quantico, concentrating on acoustic sensors and new automatic weapons. A barrel-chested, close-cropped man, he had wrestled and played football at Colorado State University and came into the Marine Corps in 1936 as an honors graduate in the Army's Reserve Officers Training Corps. A year

RECON PATROL:
A six-man heli-team complete with mortars and radioman double times out to a waiting UH-34 to join a recon mission.

Air Vice Marshal Nguyen Cao Ky —prime minister of S.Vietnam after the 1965 coup. A flamboyant fighter pilot, he effectively controlled the Saigon government in 1965-66. Elections and a new constitution then relegated him to number two position as vice-president under President Thieu. After the fall of Saigon, he fled the country, eventually opening a liquor store in the USA.

later McCutcheon followed him as an honors graduate from Carnegie Institute of Technology.

Walt took command of III MAF in a muted ceremony in the Officers Mess because the rules did not allow the outdoor display of US colors. Five days earlier, General Thi had suffered a stinging defeat. His 1st Battalion, 51st Regiment, was ambushed near Ba Gia on Route 5, which goes west from Quang Ngai city. Of the 400 men, only 65 South Vietnamese and three US advisors broke through. Thi sent in his reserves, the 39th Ranger Battalion and 3d Vietnamese Marine Battalion. They were landed by US Marine helicopters and covered by US Marine F-4B Phantoms, but were soon chewed up.

Thi, estimating the Viet Cong at five battalions, asked Saigon for two Vietnamese Airborne battalions and the help of a US Marine battalion. He got neither. Thi claimed to have killed 556 Viet Cong, but his casualties were 392 killed, wounded, and missing, and many weapons lost. In Washington the press questioned when US ground troops would go to the aid of South Vietnamese troops. On 8 June a State Department spokesman said: "American forces would be available for combat support together with Vietnamese forces when and if necessary . . ."

The *New York Times* commented: "The American people were told by a minor State Department official yesterday that, in effect, they were in a land war on the continent of Asia . . ." The White House tried to clarify the situation. The primary mission of ground troops was "to secure and safeguard important military installations like the air base at Da Nang." But, "if help is requested by the appropriate Vietnamese commander, General Westmoreland also has authority to employ these troops in support of Vietnamese forces faced with aggressive attack."

Westmoreland saw the South Vietnamese Army as being on the verge of collapse. There were now two US Army, one Australian, and seven US Marine infantry battalions in South Vietnam. Westmoreland asked that the total be brought up to 33.

On 22 June, the Joint Chiefs told Westmoreland that the number of battalions authorized for deployment to South Vietnam was 44—34 US and ten third-country, or what was now beginning to be called 'FWMAF', 'Free World Military Assistance Force.' Westmoreland was asked if he would be able, with that number, to convince the Viet Cong and North Vietnamese that they could not win. Westmoreland answered that a 44-battalion force should be able to establish a favorable balance of combat by the end of the year. Four days later he got almost unequivocal authority to "commit US troops to combat, independent or in conjunction with GVN forces . . ."

Among the new forces authorized, Westmoreland was most anxious for the arrival of the airmobile division being formed at Fort Benning, which he wished to use in the Central Highlands in II Corps Tactical Zone.

Sharp, however, did not agree that the airmobile division should go up into the Highlands; he thought it might outrun its supply lines. Taylor, too, was against the new Army division going into the mountains; believing it would invite the North Vietnamese to try for another Dien Bien Phu.

About this time the Saigon government changed. The generals ousted Dr Quat, General Nguyen Van Thieu became chief-of-state, and Air Vice Marshal Ky, Thi's adversary, de facto prime minister. Taylor viewed the new administration with distaste but wrote Ky a long letter on how to run his government, including a suggestion that he start by cleaning up the trash and garbage on Saigon's streets.

In the north, just before dawn on 1 July, a Viet Cong sapper squad broke through the wire on the east side of Da Nang air base under cover of a mortar barrage, blowing up three USAF aircraft and damaging three more. Walt was embarrassed, frustrated, and furious. No matter that the sappers had come through a part of the perimeter defended by the Vietnamese; the Washington view was that the Marines had not been able to stop a squad of sappers.

As Walt saw it, his Marines needed more room to operate. General Thi had been reluctant to use Marines in heavily populated areas and patrolling had been confined to tightly limited "tactical areas of responsibility." Under pressure from Walt, Thi agreed to extend of III MAF's TAOR to the south and east.

1st Lt. Frank Stanley Reasoner —the first of 57 Marines in Vietnam to receive the Medal of Honor. The citation for each begins 'For conspicuous gallantry and intrepidity at the risk of his life above and beyond the call of duty...' Lt. Reasoner's was awarded posthumously for his bravery while leading a reconnaissance patrol. The USS *Reasoner* was subsequently named after him.

Flowers on the Beach

HUMMINGBIRD: Helicopters quickly proved invaluable for re-supplying remote hilltop outposts. At first the Marines were severely limited in their radius of operations and not allowed to initiate combat. To secure Da Nang air base, a necklace of reconnaissance posts was set up. This one, nine miles to the northwest, had the smallest helicopter landing pad of them all. Choppers resupplied it three times a week by setting the two front wheels down and leaving the rear ones dangling over the slope.

Taylor had only agreed to be ambassador for a year while the previous ambassador, Henry Cabot Lodge, took time out for the presidential elections. Johnson and Humphrey had trounced Goldwater and Lodge in November 1964. Johnson now asked Lodge to pick up again as the US ambassador.

Westmoreland reiterated his estimate that with the help of 44 battalions, the South Vietnamese could stop losing the war in 1965, adding that with 24 more battalions in 1966 they could start winning. All contingent, of course, on what the enemy did. Defense Secretary McNamara, in shiny new chino khaki shirt and trousers, along with Taylor and Westmoreland, went north to Da Nang to visit General Thi and General Walt.

McNamara reported to President Johnson on his return and, on 28 July, Johnson announced on

television: "I have today ordered to Vietnam the Air-mobile Division and certain other forces which will raise our fighting strength from 75,000 to 125,000 almost immediately. Additional forces will be needed later, and they will be sent as requested."

General Taylor left Saigon (with a farewell medal from Thieu) on 30 July. In his last report as ambassador he told the president that the Thieu-Ky government would last out the year if the generals could stay united and the Viet Cong offensive could be blunted.

On the same day Westmoreland visited Walt at Da Nang and told him that he was to have operational control of all US ground elements in I Corps Tactical Zone, including the advisory effort and Special Forces. A week later he authorized Walt to begin offensive operations.

Waiting.

33

War for VIPs

Pacifying the villages

JET aircraft and helicopters made South Vietnam, even remote I Corps, an easy and comfortable war for Very Important Persons to visit. An unending stream of political, military, journalistic, business, theatrical, and international VIPs flowed into Da Nang.

From a few hundred feet up the war-worn city was still pastel pretty. Ships could be seen unloading at Tien Sha, and Da Nang bay was filled with picturesque bat-winged fishing boats, some bringing in cargoes other than fish.

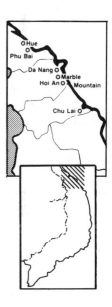

From Tien Sha the spine-tingling Marine UH-1E helicopter would swing in a great arc over the sands of China Beach as far as the jutting gray monoliths of Marble Mountain, then curve west for a deliciously low sweep along the Song Cau Do with bright green checkerboards of rice paddy on both sides. Sometimes little puffs of white smoke and the orange glint of explosions could be seen and sometimes the dull *crrummpp* of artillery heard over the pulsating roar of the Huey. Then the helicopter would gain height to fly along 'Division Ridge,' showing the red scars of Marine foxholes, and then down into Elephant Valley, where a Marine battalion protected the hamlet of Le My. 'Rural construction' was the euphemism used for 'pacification,' a term that smacked of colonialism. Landing for an obligatory visit to Le My, VIPs would be met by the tall, earnest, battalion commander who would give them a sand-table briefing, a visit to the dispensary, school, and market place, and a meeting with the village elders who, on cue, would tell tales of Viet Cong atrocities and express gratitude for all that the Americans were doing.

Afterwards, back at General Walt's quarters (he

had moved off the airfield into a sprawling dull green bungalow, built by the engineers on Division Ridge), there would be drinks and a good dinner, optimistic briefings by III MAF intelligence, operations, and civic action officers, and the positive convictions of General Walt.

The view from the general's verandah of the Bay of Da Nang was magnificent. The visitor, a day or so later, even with a stop-over in Hong Kong or Bangkok for shopping, could be back in Washington, New York, or Hollywood, filled with first-hand knowledge, possibly bemused by jet lag, of how the war would be won.

By the end of July the Marines had three regiments in I Corps—the 3d Marines west and north of Da Nang, the 9th Marines south of the city, and the 4th Marines at Chu Lai.

On 3 August a company of the 9th Marines moved up the Song Cau Do in amphibian tractors to root out a reported company of Viet Cong from Cam Ne. Like most Vietnamese villages, it was a maze of huts, bamboo, thorny hedges laced with barbed wire, and ditches lined with sharpened *punji* sticks. Met by a crackle of small arms fire, they fell back to the river, shelling the village with artillery and mortars.

They then re-entered the village followed by Columbia Broadcasting System television reporter Morley Safer. The evening CBS news showed a Marine setting fire to a hut while an old woman wailed and what the viewers would hear was Canadian-born Safer's measured irony: "If there were Viet Cong in the hamlets they were long gone."

In front of the Marines were dozens if not hundreds of 'Cam Ne's.' Under the rules of engagement from Washington and Saigon, they had to receive enemy fire before they could fire. A better way had to be found to separate the villagers from the Viet Cong infrastructure that controlled them.

Viet Cong sappers hit the Esso storage terminal at Lien Chieu on the Bay of Da Nang, north of Red Beach and halfway up Hai Van pass from the Nam O bridge, on August 5. Two million gallons of JP-4 jet fuel went up in flame and smoke. The invisibility of the enemy frustrated and perplexed the Marines. They wished that the Viet Cong would come out of the shadows, stand up, and fight. Their

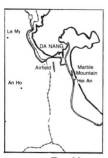

Da Nang Tactical Area of Operations 1966.

chance would come. By mid-August the 2,000-strong Viet Cong 1st Regiment moved into Van Tuong peninsula some 15 miles south of Chu Lai. The elated Marines made plans swiftly and with great secrecy.

The operation's code name was meant to be *Satellite*, but a harried clerk typed it out as *Starlite*. Colonel Oscar F. Peatross, who had been with Carlson's Raiders in World War II and one of Walt's battalion commanders in Korea, had just arrived at Chu Lai with the 7th Marines headquarters. He was given four battalions for the attack.

These converged on Van Tuong, crossing a river from the north in amphibian tractors, landing by helicopters on the west or inland side, and coming

War for VIPs

COLORADO: The downdraft from a UH-34 stirs up the dust on a landing zone after landing Marines from the 2d Bn., 5th Marines during Operation Colorado in August 1966. The 5th joined with ARVN forces in an effort to locate and destroy the NVA 2d Division near Hiep Duc in the much-fought-over Que Son Valley. The operation drove the N.Vietnamese out of the valley only for a short while.

across the beach on the southeast. In Washington, President Johnson showed a minute-by-minute interest in the battle, demanding an explanation when a column of amphibian tractors was ambushed. After six days of battle, the Marines claimed 964 Viet Cong dead at a cost of 51 dead and 203 wounded. The Viet Cong 1st Regiment was written off as combat ineffective.

But a battle such as Starlite was the exception.

As Westmoreland saw it, the Marines, having established beachheads, were reluctant to go beyond. He thought the Marines too slow, too cautious, too proprietary in their use of close air support and too bound up in amphibious doctrine.

This was a commuter's war where Westmoreland could leave his Saigon villa in the morning, fly to the battlefield in his C-123 'White Whale,' and return to his villa at night. Westmoreland was a

Westmoreland (top), an Army man, would exhort battle-weary and disheveled Marines with a list of military maxims. The Marine commander Maj. Gen. Lewis M. Walt (below) took pains to understand their problems.

frequent visitor to Walt's headquarters, where he would listen to earnest, interminable briefings arguing the Marine Corps' case for a slow, deliberate expansion of TAORs, with the Marines providing a curtain of strength behind which the fragile government of South Vietnam could strengthen and assert more positive political control sweetened with promises of a better life.

Frequently after such briefings, particularly if there had been a sharp action, Westmoreland, accompanied by Walt, would visit the Marines in the field. Typically there would be a rifle company waiting on a hillside and Westmoreland would stand in front of them in schoolmaster fashion, exhorting them with lists of maxims.

The Marines, for whom the realities of the war were heat, wetness, malaria, leeches, repetitive patrols, ambushes, sapper attacks, and antipersonnel mines that tore off a man's limbs or blew out his eyes, would sit in sweat-soaked filthy 'utilities' and listen impassively to the starched and ironed general from Saigon.

Walt, the Marines' general, had what Westmoreland lacked: the common touch. In a war in which generals were often viewed skeptically and seldom with affection, Walt, to his Marines, was 'Uncle Lew.' He restlessly roamed the sky in his command Huey, demanding impossible things of the pilot, and was never so fulfilled as when hunkered down next to a company commander or platoon leader, coaching him in the conduct of a fire-fight.

Westmoreland was scrupulously correct in his dealings with Walt and the Marines, as forebearing as he would have been in dealing with troops of a different nationality. He was acutely aware that in Washington, the Marine Commandant, General Greene, "kept a watchful eye on every sparrow," and of the special status of Krulak in Honolulu.

At the Naval Academy, Krulak, as coxswain of the varsity crew, had gotten the nickname 'the Brute.' The name stuck, partly because of his diminutive size, partly because of his deceptively quiet demeanor. As Commanding General, Fleet Marine Force, Pacific, Brute Krulak was Walt's administrative commander and not in the operational chain. But he inserted himself into operational matters in ways irksome to Westmoreland and Walt. He

VIP VISIT:
Secretary of
Defense Robert
S. McNamara
was a frequent
visitor to South
Vietnam. In
1965 he visited
ICTZ to meet
Maj. Gen.
Nguyen Chanh
Thi (left), who
later tried to
lead a violent
breakaway
from the
Saigon
government.
Jet aircraft
made it
possible for
fact-finding
visitors from
the United
States
be in Saigon in
under 24
hours.
Yet a decade
earlier French
troops had
taken nearly
three months
to get home by
sea after their
defeat in
N.Vietnam.

came to Vietnam every five to six weeks, flying in a specially configured KC-130 transport that allowed him to work and sleep in the air. The harassed III MAF staff which had to prepare for these grueling inspections called them "Krulak's monthlies." Another sort of monthly was the artful, well-illustrated report on 'Marine Operations in Vietnam' prepared at Krulak's headquarters. A copy went straight to the White House.

Krulak was a zealous guardian of the sanctity of the jointly agreed amphibious doctrine that governed Marine Corps landings and the Marine Corps' deeply-felt doctrine on the use of its fixed-winged tactical aircraft. Marine Corps and Air Force tactical air doctrine differed fundamentally: the Air Force believed that all tactical aviation should be under centralized Air Force operational control. The Marine Corps believed equally vehemently that its tactical aircraft were best used as an integrated supporting arm, like artillery or tanks, and that control should remain with the Marine commander. Krulak, Walt, and McCutcheon had bitter memories

War for VIPs

GUARD & RESCUE:
A UH-34 hovers above the battle zone to make an emergency medical evacuation, as a Marine M-48 tank stands guard during Operation Starlite south of Chu Lai. Throughout the operation, the first regimental-size US action, choppers from Marine Aircraft Group 16 dropped into the fields to pick up wounded, frequently within 50 yards of fierce fighting. In keeping with Marine tradition no request from the fiercely-engaged ground troops was ever refused.

of Marine tactical air under control of the Fifth Air Force in Korea.

When the first Marine F-4 squadron had arrived in April, Westmoreland wanted it under the operational control of Air Force General Moore, his deputy commander for air. Admiral Sharp, however, knowing the Marines' sensitivity and with a probable nudge from Krulak, ruled that Moore's authority be limited to coordination. McCutcheon, as Walt's

deputy commander for air, worked out a MACV directive that acknowledged Moore as the coordinating authority but retained operational control of Marine aviation under Walt. III MAF was, however, to notify 2d Air Division of any excess aircraft so that these sorties could be allocated elsewhere.

Moore wanted operational control of all air defense, but McCutcheon pointed out that the F-4

A Kit Carson scout and a Marine consult over enemy locations. Named after the Western hero who guided the US Cavalry through Indian country, Kit Carson scouts were frequently defectors from the Viet Cong who had been persuaded to switch sides and then given eight weeks special training.

was capable of both close support and air defense. It was agreed that McCutcheon would designate those Marine forces that would participate in air defense, which would also include the Hawk batteries. The agreement, signed in August and unchanged until 1968, rankled Westmoreland.

Westmoreland was also not enamored with the Marines' pacification strategy enunciated by Krulak and practiced by Walt. However, he knew only too well that many hamlets and villages, nominally under government control, could not pass the simple acid test: "Does the chief sleep there at night?"

The security of hamlets and villages largely rested with two levels of militia: the Popular Force and the Regional Force. The diagrams on situation maps showed a locally-recruited PF squad for every hamlet, a PF platoon for every village, and an RF company at every district headquarters. Reality was less impressive.

The Popular Forces were at the bottom of Vietnamese priorities. Weapons were scarce, chiefly carbines and grenades. Uniforms were seldom provided so the usual garb was a black-market set of Army fatigues cut down to skin tightness and worn with a bush hat.The Regional Forces were scarcely better off. The Marines, with dim tribal memories of white-officered native constabularies in Haiti, Nicaragua, and the Dominican Republic, groped for means of improving their Vietnamese equivalents.

The five villages edging the Phu Bai enclave each had a Popular Force platoon. After several near disasters caused by lack of effective communication, the 3d Battalion, 4th Marines, formed a 'Joint Action Company' (later changed to a more accurately named 'Combined Action Company') of volunteers and from it assigned a squad of Marines and a Navy hospital corpsman to work with the PF platoons. The Marines entered into village life, offered rudimentary health care, training in weapons and tactics, and brought assured communications, supply, and fire support. Command relations were hazy, dependent upon cooperation between PF platoon leaders and Marine squad leaders, but the system seemed to work. When the battalion commander was transferred to Da Nang to take command of 3d Battalion, 9th Marines, which then had the task of airfield security, he brought the CAC concept with him and applied it to neighborhoods close to the base. Thi approved a further extension of the TAOR south of Da Nang but urged caution "to avoid deplorable incidents to the local people." By the end of the month, the 9th Marines had advanced a third of the way to Hoi An and had 'cleared' the nine villages of Hoa Vang district. Disturbed by the amount of rice apparently going over to the Viet Cong, the regiment began to protect the harvest with Operation Golden Fleece, chiefly by putting cordons of Marines around the harvesters during the day patrolling extensively at night to disrupt illicit trafficking in rice.

On 27 October, Viet Cong raiders hit the Marble Mountain Air Facility, the new base for MAG-16 and its helicopters on China Beach. Sappers, stripped down to undershorts, reached the helicopter parking pad and with bangalore torpedoes and bundles of grenades knocked out 24 aircraft and damaged 23 more. The Marines counted 41 Viet Cong dead and lost three killed and 91 wounded.

That same night the Viet Cong also hit the SATS strip at Chu Lai. Only two Viet Cong made it to MAG-11's flight line but, before being killed, they blew up two A-4 Skyhawks and damaged six more.

At the end of October, the energetic ARVN lieutenant colonel who was the Quang Nam province chief unveiled his plan, *Ngu Hanh Son,* or the 'Nine Village Program,' to complete the pacification of Hoa Vang district. It was something of a carbon copy of Hop Tac, but to III MAF Marines it seemed new and promising. The pacification of the five villages (including troublesome Cam Ne) west of Highway One would come first. Then the effort would shift to the east of the highway. The specially organized 59th Regional Force Battalion would provide security.

In Central Annam the monsoon is the reverse of the rest of South Vietnam. It blows from the northeast and as it crosses the China Sea picks up moisture. Clouds form, to be driven against the Annamite mountains, and the rains begin. They were expected in September but in 1965 did not come until October. By November they were averaging an inch of rain a day. Canvas turned green and moldy; the wind-roughened sea made unloading difficult; the red laterite roads dissolved into thin greasy mud; rain, drizzle, and clouds filled the valleys; tempers shortened.

RICE BULLION:
Two Marines load bags of rice into a LVT as part of Operation Golden Fleece. Marine commanders were disturbed by the amount of rice reaching the Viet Cong and set out to disrupt the trafficking by cordoning the fields during harvest and taking rice under armed guard to market.

Chasing Charlie

THE Viet Cong 1st Regiment, its ranks miraculously refilled after the losses suffered in Starlite, advanced out of the mountains of western Quang Tin on 16 November, overrunning the Regional Force garrison at Hiep Duc, a district headquarters in the valley of the Song Thu Bon. Hiep Duc was in the ARVN 2d Division's zone and Thi pushed the decision as to a counterattack onto Brigadier General Hoang Xuan Lam, the division commander. Thi was called the 'Warlord of the North,' but his writ did not extend entirely into Quang Tin and Quang Ngai provinces. These were the fiefdom of Lam. Unlike the wiry and catlike Thi, Lam was physically a big man for a Vietnamese, rather heavy, with a moon face and a habit of chuckling before speaking so that the Marines referred to him privately as 'Ho Ho.'

The next day, Lam sent two battalions of his 5th Regiment to retake Hiep Duc. The Marine UH-34s that lifted them had to corkscrew down through the monsoon clouds and rain into a tiny landing zone. Worse, the Viet Cong had rimmed the valley with 12.7mm antiaircraft machine guns, the first time the Marines met these weapons in numbers. Marine F-4s and A-4s roared down through the gray-white clouds to take out the guns, but, even so, 20 of the 30 helicopters took hits.

The town was recaptured. Thi and Lam faced a bitter choice: garrison Hiep Duc with at least a battalion of regulars or pull back. Whose decision it was is not clear, but Marine helicopters went whirring back through the monsoon skies to take out the two battalions.

On 22 November the North Vietnamese 18th Regiment attacked Thach Tru, an earthen fort 29 kilometers south of Quang Ngai city on Highway

One. The attackers did not know that the normal garrison of two Regional Force companies had been joined by the 37th Ranger Battalion. Even so they got through the wire and over the palisade into the fort, closing with the defenders in bloody hand-to-hand fighting. Luckily only one Ranger company was penned up in the fort. Another company was in the village and a third on a hill overlooking the fort. US advisors with the Rangers on the hill called for

Chasing Charlie

PADDY WAR:
The Marines were at their most exposed traversing rice paddies. A walk in the tropical sun could quickly change into a tropical hell. Here a Marine column with too little interval between men, crosses a paddy south of Da Nang using a paddy dike, often the location of antipersonnel mines. Above a door gunner in a UH-34, with his machine gun at the ready, watches for enemy activity from the treeline just passed by the column.

naval support. Two US destroyers, *O'Brien* and *Bache,* pumped in 5-inch shells until the attackers pulled back toward the western hills. In mid-afternoon a US Marine battalion thundered in by helicopter, while an armored column from Lam's division came down the highway. The attackers left behind 175 dead.

McNamara arrived in Saigon to discuss with Westmoreland the arrival of such uniformed North

49

PARTING GIFT: Gen. Nguyen Chanh Thi presents a captured Viet Cong submachine gun to Marine Corps commandant Gen. Wallace M. Greene in January '66. Thi, effectively the warlord in control of central Vietnam south of the DMZ, would be deposed two months later by Air Vice Marshal Ky and placed under house arrest in Saigon for attempting an alliance with the militant Buddhist opposition leaders.

Vietnamese. Westmoreland had his 44 battalions, but the MACV order of battle showed the enemy with 110 battalions, of which 27 were North Vietnamese. Westmoreland had a new set of requirements for McNamara. By the end of 1966 he wanted in the field 162 ARVN battalions, 74 US battalions, and 23 other Free World battalions—bringing US troop strength up to about 400,000. McNamara accepted his estimates and told Johnson to be prepared to accept a thousand Americans killed in action each month.

The abandonment of Hiep Duc had left open the west gate to Que Son valley. The Viet Cong 1st Regiment pressed forward in its almost invisible way, threatening the garrisons of Viet An and Que Son, two more district headquarters. General Walt offered Thi a coordinated operation: a Vietnamese regiment would move into the valley by the road that ran from Thang Binh on Highway One to Que Son and then on to Viet An and Hiep Duc. When the South Vietnamese developed a solid contact, two US battalions would go in by helicopter behind the enemy. A third US Marine battalion would be in reserve. The complicated operation was called "Harvest Moon". The command group of the ARVN 5th Regiment, which had done well at Hiep Duc, moved out early on 8 December with two battalions, its 1st Battalion on the left of the road and the 11th Ranger Battalion on the right. The 11th Rangers marched straight into the sleeve of a Viet Cong ambush. The 1st Battalion faced around but could not get across the road to help. When Marine helicopters brought in the ARVN 1st Battalion, 6th Regiment, the Viet Cong faded away, but attacked the next morning, killing the regimental commander. Regimental headquarters dissolved.

1st Lt. Harvey C. Barnum, Jr. —received the Congressional Medal of Honor for his bravery while serving as a forward artillery observer in Quang Tri province in December 1966. He was later promoted to the rank of colonel.

Then US Marines entered the battle. The 2d Battalion, 7th Marines, landed west of the line of contact while 3d Battalion, 3d Marines, moved between the Viet Cong and the now-shattered 1st Battalion, 5th Regiment. Task Force Delta, a provisional Marine headquarters, and several batteries of artillery were helilifted into Que Son and the fight continued. The next day the Seventh Fleet's Special Landing Force—2d Battalion, 1st Marines—landed well into the valley. Walt, growing impatient, relieved the Task Force Delta commander and gave command to newly-arrived Brigadier General Jonas M. Platt, one of his battalion commanders in Korea.

Westmoreland's J-3, the feisty and aggressive Brigadier General William E. DePuy, USA, suggested using B-52s. The first B-52 strike was delivered 12 December. General Walt watched the rain of bombs from his helicopter and sent a message to Strategic Air Command: "We are more than impressed with the results; we are delighted."

General Lam, unmistakeable in his tanker's black beret and silver badges, gathered up his shaken battalions. Most of the South Vietnamese listed as 'missing' had returned and were sent up into the hills, where the B-52s had struck. Soon the Viet Cong 1st Regiment had disappeared again.

Brig. Gen. (later Maj. Gen.) William DePuy —suggested using B-52s.

Westmoreland demanded an explanation of the battle and the international press in Saigon, smelling dissension, spoke of a trap baited with ARVN troops that failed to close.

With the beginning of the New Year the North

Vietnamese 325A Division seemed to be bent on the classic maneuver of separating the northern five provinces from the South, advancing along the axis of the border separating Quang Ngai and Binh Dinh provinces, which was also the boundary between the I and II Corps Tactical Zones. Westmoreland ordered the highly mobile 1st Cavalry Division to go after the 325A Division in Binh Dinh province.

To the north, Platt's Task Force Delta in a coordinated operation, Double Eagle, landed two battalions on 28 January from the sea 20 miles south of the town of Quang Ngai and helilifted another battalion into the hills behind the beachhead.

Premier Ky and the beautiful Mrs. Ky, dressed in black flight suits, velvet caps, lavender chiffon scarves, and white gauntlets, made a dazzling visit

LANDING ZONE:
Marine riflemen fan out at the double after a helidrop into the battle area.

For the Marines 1966 opened with a series of operations along the coast of ICTZ between Hue and Quang Ngai.

to the beachhead. Ky's 'government of generals' was surviving but not acquiring wide support. Ky estimated that it controlled no more than 25 percent of the population.

Johnson wanted to size up Ky personally. The Honolulu Conference, a pivotal meeting, was held at Sharp's headquarters from 6 to 8 February 1966. It ended with a joint communique that emphasized winning the war through military action and expanded civic reforms.

A day or so before going to Honolulu Westmoreland met Walt at Da Nang. His J-2 estimated that there were 22 enemy battalions in Quang Tri and Thua Thien. Westmoreland was convinced that a major offensive was coming, probably aimed at taking Hue. Walt thought otherwise. His G-2 credited the enemy with only nine battalions where the MACV J-2 saw 22. Walt's guess was that if the North Vietnamese did attack it would be against the border outposts and Special Forces camps. He saw no great threat to Hue. A Marine battalion and a Marine helicopter squadron at Phu Bai were the only American forces north of the Hai Van pass, but the ARVN 1st Division, commanded by the highly regarded Brigadier General Nguyen Van Chuan, was in the northern two provinces.

Westmoreland ordered Walt to prepare contingency plans to meet an invasion from Laos or across the DMZ.

Walt left Da Nang on 10 February for a month's temporary duty in Washington. There were consultations with the Joint Chiefs and a surprise promotion by President Johnson to lieutenant general. While he was gone, his Marines battled the Viet Cong 810th Main Force Battalion northeast of Phu Bai and linked up with Lam's 2d Division against the PAVN 36th Regiment northwest of Quang Ngai City. Both fights went well, with a gratifying body count and a good number of captured weapons.

When Walt returned to Da Nang he found a real threat to Hue, but from a different quarter than Westmoreland had anticipated. Thich Tri Quang, he of the "staring eyes and shining white teeth" and leader of the militant Buddhists, had left the sanctuary of the Saigon pagodas and had gone to Hue. Ky suspected that he had made an alliance with Thi, whom Ky saw as a separatist, possibly to the point of taking Annam out of the war. On 10 March Ky convened the National Leadership Council. By secret ballot the generals voted Thi's dismissal on the grounds of insubordination. General Chuan was given command of I Corps and Brigadier General Pham Xuan Nhuan was given the ARVN 1st Division. It was announced that Thi had gone on sick leave.

Thi was under house arrest in Saigon. On 12 March, 2000 marchers, many ARVN soldiers in uniform, demonstrated in Da Nang. The pro-Thi, anti-Ky groups coalesced into a 'Military-Civilian Struggle Group.' Next day a general strike was called and by 15 March Da Nang and Hue were pretty much shut down. To ease the situation Thi was allowed to return to his official residence in Hue with his promise that he would accept his dismissal.

Meanwhile the string of Special Forces camps that diagrammed so well on the maps as an outpost line, blocking or at least screening entries from Laos, was crumbling.

In December the South Vietnamese had closed A Loui and Ta Bat, two of the three CIDG camps in critical A Shau valley west of Hue. A Shau, the remaining camp, came under North Vietnamese attack in March. A drenching by mortar shells cost the defenders 57 casualties. The garrison was a battalion of Montagnard irregulars, a company of Nung mercenaries, and a command group of Vietnamese Special Forces and their American Special Forces counterparts. An Air Force AC-47 'Puff the Magic Dragon' gunship coming to their support was shot down. A Marine helicopter taking out wounded was lost.

The North Vietnamese attacked from two sides. The defense at the southeast corner collapsed and the attackers swarmed into the camp. The remaining defenders were forced into a pocket along the inside of the palisaded north wall. Two Marine A-4 Skyhawks attempted close support under the light of flares dropped by an Air Force C-123. One A-4 was lost.

At daylight a flight of prop-driven A-1E Skyraiders came overhead. One was hit by ground fire and made a forced landing on A Shau's fire-swept dirt airstrip. Flight leader Major Bernard F. Fisher, USAF, landed his own A-1E, took off the downed

1963
The chain of Special Forces outposts designed to guard the border with Laos quickly crumbled between 1963 and 1964.

1964

Chasing Charlie

FIELD COMMANDER: Maj. Gen. Lewis W. Walt, then commanding both the 3d Marine Division and the III Marine Amphibious Force, confers with a company commander during Operation Harvest Moon in the Que Son valley in 1966. A much-decorated World War II and Korean war hero, Walt was one of the most accessible field commanders, preferring first-hand reports to paperwork.

pilot, and later received a Medal of Honor. In Da Nang, Lieutenant General John Heintges, Westmoreland's deputy ground commander, agreed with Walt to evacuate A Shau. The burden fell to Lieutenant Colonel Charles House's HMM-163 flying the obsolescent UH-34.

The Nungs, of Chinese ethnic origin and like the Gurkhas in their martial tradition, were attempting to hold the landing zone. Enemy fire was heavy. Panicky irregulars had to be shot by US Green

USAF Maj. Bernard F. Fisher —landed his Skyraider under fire on a dirt air strip at A Shau to rescue a fellow pilot. He later received the Medal of Honor for this act of gallantry.

Berets and Marine crewmen to keep them from overloading the rescuing helicopters. House's and one other helicopter crashed. House organized his crew and about 50 Vietnamese into a makeshift force and led them off into the jungle to await rescue. Next day they were found by Marine helicopters. For his efforts, House received a Navy Cross and a letter of reprimand.

The fall of A Shau gave substance to Westmoreland's concerns for Hue. Walt moved the 4th

Lt. Col. Charles A.House —After his helicopter and another crashed during the fall of A Shau, he led his crew and a column of Vietnamese into the jungle to await rescue. His actions earned him a Navy Cross and a letter of reprimand.

F-8E Crusader single-seat used by the Marines in a ground attack role.

Marines from Chu Lai north to Phu Bai, where they would be close at hand to the ancient capital, which still had some of the aspects of an open city. Major General Wood B. Kyle, a veteran of Guadalcanal, Tarawa, Saipan, and Tinian, had arrived to take command of the 3d Marine Division. Two-thirds of the 1st Marine Division were also in place with its commander, Major General Lewis J. Fields.

There were reports of an enemy build-up around the CIDG camp at Khe Sanh, on Route 9 in Quang Tin province about four miles east of the Laotian border. Westmoreland, always prodding the Marines to get out of their 'beachheads,' ordered Walt to send a battalion to Khe Sanh to 'search-and-destroy.' Walt did not like to send his battalions thrashing about the green hills against vanishing targets.

Furthermore, the Buddhist troubles were not yet over. Demonstrators seized the radio stations in Hue and Da Nang. Walt and his staff, watching and listening, saw to their dismay the countryside being abandoned to the Viet Cong as the ARVN pulled back into the cities. A parade through Hue on 3 April by 3,000 members of the ARVN 1st Division, marching to the beat of the Division band and calling for the overthrow of the Ky-Thieu government, demonstrated how far the defection had gone.

In Hue, General Nhuan, commanding the ARVN 1st Division, declared himself and his division on the side of Thi and the Struggle Force. All the 'non-essential' US civilians were evacuated from the imperial city.

A Struggle Force mechanized column started up Highway One from Hoi An toward Da Nang. Walt's Marines were ordered to stop them. A company of the 9th Marines threw up a road block at Thanh Quit bridge, nine miles south of the field. The two forces glared at each other. The colonel commanding the Struggle Force ordered a battery of four 155mm guns to be unlimbered and laid on the air base. A flight of Marine F-8E Crusaders came overhead. A Marine lieutenant poked a finger under the nose of the Vietnamese colonel and said, "One round—just one round, and we take you out."

Next day, 10 April, Ky sent his own man, Lieutenant General Ton That Dinh, north to relieve Chuan as corps commander. Thieu, speaking for the Directorate, promised elections in from three to five months. The Buddhists appeared mollified but their leader, Tri Quang, was insistent that Ky step down.

Bad weather and the political situation had given Walt an excuse to procrastinate on Westmoreland's order to send a battalion to Khe Sanh. It was not until 17 April that the 1st Battalion, 1st Marines, landed at the CIDG camp in Marine KC-130s. The battalion commander, Lieutenant Colonel Van D. 'Ding Dong' Bell, a one-time middleweight boxer, set up his command post in a tea plantation and patrolled the difficult hills, provoking no enemy reaction except for a single ineffective sniper shot. He ended the operation with a flourish: a march-out along Route 9 to Dong Ha, where the battalion was greeted by Westmoreland and Walt.

Ky stirred up the Buddhists by announcing that the promised elections would be for a Constituent Assembly only, to draft a new constitution, not to elect a National Assembly. Tri Quang reacted violently and once again the saffron-robed monks and white-shirted students were out in the streets.

On 15 May rickety Vietnamese C-47 transports shuttled two Airborne and two Marine battalions north to Da Nang. Their first objective was I Corps headquarters at the edge of the field. Dinh made an ignominious escape and a mad dash in a jeep to Walt's headquarters, where he asked for sanctuary.

Ky's paratroopers and Marines then fanned out through the city, arrested the mayor, and, with the practice of past coups, occupied the city hall, police headquarters, radio station, and other centers of civic control. The rebels, however, still held a good part of the city, including the principal pagodas and most of Tien Sha peninsula, vital to port operations and the logistics heart of I Corps.

A reluctant Major General Huynh Can Cao arrived to be corps commander in place of the absentee Ton That Dinh. Cao, a Catholic, was hardly a choice to placate the Buddhists. A visit to the headquarters of the ARVN 1st Division in Hue ended in a fire-fight in which a Vietnamese lieutenant was killed.

In Da Nang, Walt was pummeled with telephone calls from Washington. Pulling the American forces back into their enclaves was considered. Some strong voices in the government argued for complete withdrawal.

The street fighting in Da Nang continued. The

Lt. Col. Van D. 'Ding Dong' Bell —led the first battalion of Marines into Khe Sanh in April 1966 after Westmoreland insisted on a search-and-destroy mission that proved fruitless.

His M-16 rifle at the ready, a Marine moves through the rubble-strewn streets of Hue. Streetfighting in Hue called for a new kind of combat similar to the 1st Marine Division's fight for Seoul in the Korean War. Without the advantage of their superior mobility and firepower the Marine infantry had to fight street by street taking out a sniper at a time to win control of the city.

Vietnamese Marines reached the bridge over to Tien Sha peninsula and found its Struggle Force defenders prepared to blow it up. General Walt went to the bridge and in a bit of histrionics faced down the defenders and got the demolition charges removed.

In best Buddhist style, the pagodas became the main centers of resistance, particularly Tien Hoa pagoda, where 350 rebels held out under the multicolored Buddhist flag. Cao rolled up his tanks but hesitated to blast away at the pagoda. Colonel Ngoc Loan, whom Ky had just named as the new head of the National Police, leveled his pistol at Cao's head and ordered him to attack. (This is the same Colonel Loan who later figured in one of the most famous photos of the war, blowing out the brains of a Viet Cong suspect on the streets of Saigon.) Cao eluded Loan and, following Dinh's example, raced to Walt's headquarters and asked for asylum and safe passage to the United States.

Next day Ky countermanded the order to attack the pagoda. He called the pistol-happy Loan to Saigon and found another general, Du Quoc Dong, to take over as acting I Corps commander. At Tien Sha the rebels still held a large ammunition dump, which they threatened to blow up. Ky sent a flight of A-1 Skyraiders in after the defenders. This was too much for Walt and he put up a flight of Marine jet fighters to hold off any further South Vietnamese air attacks. On 23 May, after much rhetoric, the dump was turned over to the US Marines and Tien Sha pagoda surrendered.

Westmoreland convinced Thi that the time had come for him to come to terms with Ky. The two adversaries met at Chu Lai. Thi agreed to go to Da Lat to await 'reassignment' (and eventual exile to the United States). The leopard had won over the tiger. Lam, the durable commander of the ARVN 2d Division, was now given command of I Corps.

Thi was finished, but, in Hue, Tri Quang was still active and there were more riots, more destruction, and a second evacuation of American noncombatants. The US consulate was drenched with gasoline and burned.

On 10 June 300 National Police under the personal command of Colonel Loan were airlifted into the city. Four loyal battalions motor-marched north

HUMPERS:
A 3d Marine Division 81mm mortar platoon hump forward under their heavy load during Operation Double Eagle, fought south of Chu Lai in early 1966. The 81mm, a medium mortar, weighed over 110 lbs and could be broken down into three sections. Its range was from 100 meters up to 3,650 meters with a fire rate of up to 20 rounds per minute.

from Da Nang. The column reached Hue on 12 June. More tear gas than bullets was used in breaking the last centers of resistance—the Citadel and two near-by pagodas. Nhuan was ousted and Tri Quang was put into a Saigon hospital where he promptly went on a hunger strike.

Vietnamese casualties were at least 150 killed and 700 wounded, but the greatest casualty was the pacification effort—brought to a cold stop.

Defending the DMZ

WESTMORELAND, attempting to fight a coherent war against a background of domestic political chaos, was convinced the next North Vietnamese move would be across the DMZ. Once again at Westmoreland's prodding, Walt sent a battalion north to reconnoiter, this time to work out of Dong Ha. The battalion arrived on 30 May, found no enemy, and returned to Phu Bai.

In mid-June, Westmoreland ordered Walt to repeat his reconnaissance. The 4th Marines established a patrol base at Dong Ha. Prisoners taken by the ARVN made it clear that the PAVN or NVA 324B Division was south of the DMZ with the mission of 'liberating' Quang Tin. On 4 July a Marine patrol working 16 miles west of Dong Ha found fresh earth-works on a 700-foot needle of rock that would come to be called 'the Rockpile.'

Task Force Delta was reactivated, under the command of Brigadier General Lowell English, and given four infantry battalions, an artillery battalion, and assorted reinforcements. Dong Ha, located where Route 9 intersects with Highway One and where the Song Cua Viet comes in from the sea, would be the logistic support area and airhead. English, assistant division commander of the 3d Marine Division, would have his command post at Cam Lo, seven miles to the west. Between Dong Ha and Cam Lo the ground was fairly level and open. North of Cam Lo were rolling hills covered with scrub growth. To the west the hills got higher, the vegetation thicker, and the terrain tougher.

Intelligence put the headquarters of the 324B Division and its 90th Regiment, some 1,500 men, in the valley of the Song Ngan, six miles north of Cam Lo. English helicoptered two battalions of Marines into

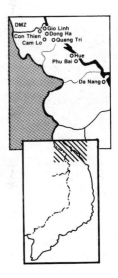

Defending the DMZ

ROCKPILE TIPTOE: The Rockpile, an isolated outcrop of jagged rock near the western edge of the DMZ, provided the Marines with a crucial observation and communication site.

It could only be re-supplied by tippy-toe landings with supplies unloaded hurriedly while the pilot stayed at full throttle in case the landing zone came under gunfire.

Song Ngan, which ran into heavy resistance at the river. The North Vietnamese regular was a different breed—a tough, orthodox light infantryman well-equipped with Chinese-made assault rifles, automatic weapons, and mortars.

The North Vietnamese main body seemed to be somewhere in the triangle formed by Cam Lo, the Song Ngan, and the Rockpile. The Special Landing Force battalion was landed in the center of the triangle while the two battalions from the Song

Ngan marched south. The enemy moved west and the Marines pressed after him, fighting a last heavy action against a battalion dug in on Hill 364. About 8,000 Marines, including five infantry battalions, had been in contact and some 3,000 ARVN had been in the companion action. The Marines had lost 126 killed, 448 wounded; the ARVN 21 killed, 40 wounded. Enemy killed were calculated at 824. Task Force Delta was deactivated, and except for one battalion, departed to fight elsewhere.The 2d Battalion, 4th

Capt. Howard V. Lee —received the Medal of Honor for his bravery while commanding a company at Cam Lo in August 1966. Later promoted to rank of colonel.

Marines remained divided between two bases, Dong Ha and Cam Lo, with an outpost on the Rockpile. 'Stingray' teams—four or five highly trained reconnaissance Marines to a team—screened the front.

Walt still saw the NVA actions along the DMZ as a diversion to draw US forces away from pacification efforts. Westmoreland was equally convinced that the 324B Division, bloodied but far from beaten, was still south of the DMZ and that two more NVA divisions, the 304th and 341st, were staging just north of the DMZ—portending a major North Vietnamese invasion.

Stingray Team 'Groucho Marx' sighted an NVA patrol two miles north of the Rockpile on 6 August and called in artillery fire. Fire missions continued for the next two days; then it was time to extricate the surrounded team. First a platoon, then a company, were fed in to cover the extraction and it became a bitter fight with a North Vietnamese battalion. The new operation was called "Prairie."

The 1st Battalion, 4th Marines, was sent to Cam Lo and by the third week in August it was clear that the North Vietnamese had occupied a ridgeline, 'Razorback,' 1,000 meters north of the Rockpile. 2d Battalion, 4th Marines, cleared Razorback at a cost of ten percent of its strength. The single prisoner captured by the Marines said his regiment, the 803d, after first taking the Rockpile, was to swing east and join another regiment against Cam Lo.

The attack against Cam Lo, weakened by the absence of the 803d, came on 26 August. Some North Vietnamese got through the wire and there was a wild two hours of hunting them down. Again just one prisoner was taken, from the 812th Regiment.

Another battalion was added to Prairie and the Marines moved north from Cam Lo to Con Thien, up against the edge of the DMZ. Reconnaissance confirmed that the 324B Division's third infantry regiment, the 90th, was also present.

To see just how strong the enemy was in the eastern end of the zone, the Special Landing Force battalion, coming mainly from helicopter carrier *Iwo Jima* and covered by the 8-inch guns of heavy cruiser *St. Paul,* landed on 15 September and swept westward. The SLF stayed ashore ten days, took a heavy 203 casualties, and claimed 200 enemy killed. Meanwhile the North Vietnamese had gotten back onto Razorback and a fresh battalion was sent to drive them off. The hardest fighting was for Hills 400 and 484. Among the Marine dead was a company commander, Captain James J. Carroll, whose name would be given to a new artillery base just west of Cam Lo.

The rules of the war gave the North Vietnamese sanctuary against ground action until they emerged from the DMZ. How then to defend the northern reaches? Westmoreland ruled out a World War I trenchline from the China Sea to Laos as being impossibly expensive in manpower and decided on a 'strong-point obstacle system': fire support and patrol bases such as were already evolving to channel enemy advances into killing zones, where they could be hit with air and artillery and counterattacked with mobile reserves.

Westmoreland saw Gio Linh, the town where Highway One crossed into the DMZ, and Con Thien as being the most important forward bases. Behind came the string of armed camps along Route 9, including Cam Lo, Camp Carroll, the Rockpile, and on the left flank, at the end of the line, Khe Sanh.

In mid-September, Westmoreland went to the Philippines to meet with Lieutenant General Alfred D. Starbird, USA, who had plans from McNamara's scientific advisors for an anti-infiltration barrier. Its heart was electronic sensors, supposedly marvellous devices which could translate disturbance or movement into electrical signals transmitted back to an observer's console. These sensors mixed liberally with antipersonnel mines would be sown in belts of barbed wire (of new West German design using razor-blade edges) connecting the fortified camps. Installing the barrier would be a monumental engineering task: bulldozing a cleared swath from the sea to Laos and then installing the system.

However, the defense of the DMZ could not wait. Westmoreland admired the fighting qualities of the Marines but considered them tactically and logistically obtuse. He ordered the construction of a new airfield at Quang Tri and the development of unloading facilities along the Cua Viet so that resupply would not be choked off if the monsoons or enemy closed Hai Van pass. To ease Walt's concern over the thinning of the pacification effort, he

Northern Quang Tri province. —The Camp Carroll artillery base near Cam Lo was named after Capt. James J. Carroll, who was killed during the fighting to clear the NVA from the Razorback, a ridgeline 1,000m north of the Rockpile.

Defending the DMZ

ROCKET ATTACK: A Marine of Company M, 3d Battalion, 4th Marines moves cautiously forward with a 3.5-inch rocket round in his hands while two other Marines work with their radio and compass. This was in Operation Prairie near the DMZ in late September 1966. The Prairie series of operations would go on until 31 May 1967, and see some of the heaviest fighting of the war.

temporarily redeployed a battalion of the 173d Airborne Brigade to Da Nang. To make up for the Marines' deficiency in artillery, he moved an artillery group headquarters to the north, sending with it an Army self-propelled 105mm howitzer battalion. He also ordered a battalion of the US Army's new 175mm guns positioned at Camp Carroll, speaking glowingly to Walt about the gun's 20-mile range and great accuracy.

Westmoreland was particularly concerned over

what he considered to be Walt's failure to grasp the significance of Khe Sanh. He feared that with the Marines preoccupied with the 324B Division in the center and east of the sector, the other two North Vietnamese divisions would sweep around the Marines' left flank and take the CIDG-Special Forces camp.

Khe Sanh was more than just a patrol base screening infiltration from Laos along Route 9. It was also the base for still-secret operations into Laos and its

175mm gun —The longest range artillery weapon of the war, it could fire a 147 lb. shell 20 miles. Although the high command in Saigon had great hopes for its use in outlying firebases, it proved a costly and time-consuming disappointment.

airstrip was also used by gunships interdicting the Ho Chi Minh trail.

The Marines continued to discount the military importance of Khe Sanh. As General English put it: "When you're at Khe Sanh, you're really not anywhere . . . You could lose it and you really haven't lost a damn thing."

But Walt reluctantly moved the 1st Battalion, 3d Marines, to Khe Sanh. The CIDG and Special Forces, in turn, relocated to a new camp at Lang Vei, a few miles further to the west.

Six Marine infantry battalions—two-thirds of a division—were now in Quang Tri province. English had under him two regimental headquarters. The 4th Marines controlled the eastern half, including Dong Ha, Con Thien, and Cam Lo. The 3d Marines had the center, including Camp Carroll and the Rockpile. Khe Sanh remained directly under English. Walt now ordered Kyle to move the 3d Marine Division headquarters north from Da Nang to Phu Bai and to set up a forward command post at Dong Ha.

The northeast monsoon was blowing. Western Quang Tri was unexpectedly cold and dank. Engineers worried about Route 9, mostly dirt-topped, standing up to military traffic.

The expected North Vietnamese onslaught never came off. By November, intelligence was reporting that the 324B Division had retired north of the DMZ. Prairie I was declared over on 31 January 1967. A body count of 1,397 enemy killed, 27 captured, went into the computers. The Marines' losses were 239 killed, 1,214 wounded.

English went home and Brigadier General Michael P. Ryan, holder of a Navy Cross from Tarawa, took command. Detecting large concentrations of enemy men and material north of the Ben Hai river, he gained permission to fire into and north of the DMZ itself.

The North Vietnamese reacted with increased artillery and heavy mortar fire against Con Thien and Gio Linh. Reconnaissance confirmed that leading elements of 324B Division were once again south of the DMZ. The North Vietnamese brought in a new weapon, spin-stabilized 122mm rockets, to bombard the Marine camps. The heaviest fighting, mostly in rolling grasslands, came in the 3d Marines' sector, now commanded by Colonel John P. Lanigan. Two fresh Marine battalions were fed into the fight and the enemy once again withdrew. Prairie II ended 18 March. The NVA had lost 694 killed and 20 captured. The Marines had lost 93 killed, 483 wounded.

On 20 March, General Kyle, his year in Vietnam completed, was replaced as Commanding General, 3d Marine Division, by Major General Bruno A. Hochmuth, a tall, 56-year-old Texan. That same day Con Thien and Gio Linh were pounded by 1,000 rounds of artillery, mortar, and rocket fire.

It was quite clear that elements of the 324B and 341st Divisions were still south of the Ben Hai. Walt's greatest concern was that the North Vietnamese might overrun his artillery base at Gio Linh, which included a battery of the vaunted 175mm guns. (The 175mm gun, with its slow rate of fire, wide dispersion at great ranges, and short barrel life, was to prove a major disappointment.)

Walt got Westmoreland's permission to bring in the Special Landing Force for a sweep of the sandy wastes east of Gio Linh. The SLF, now the 1st Battalion, 4th Marines, came ashore on 20 March, made solid contact the next day, and in a week's fighting killed 334 enemy at a cost of 29 Marines killed, 230 wounded. Prairie III ground on until 19 April, costing the North Vietnamese 252 killed and the Marines 56 killed and 530 wounded.

Westmoreland deployed Army Task Force Oregon to Quang Ngai and Quang Tin, allowing Walt to move his two Marine divisions entirely into the northern three provinces. This included shifting the 9th Marines, after two years in Quang Nam, to Quang Tri. The 9th Marines set up headquarters at Dong Ha; the 3d Marines' command post was at Camp Carroll; and the 4th Marines, with its headquarters at Phu Bai, concentrated on counter-guerrilla operations in Thua Thien.

The Marine garrison at Khe Sanh had been reduced to a rifle company. On 24 April a platoon, patrolling five miles west of the base, encountered an enemy force, which after initial hesitation, smashed into them.

Next day, the 3d Battalion, 3d Marines, was flown into Khe Sanh and became heavily engaged with what seemed to be an enemy battalion entrenched on Hill 861. Colonel Lanigan now took personal

Maj. Gen. Bruno A. Hochmuth —commanded the 3d Marine Division from 20 March 1967, until his death eight months later in a helicopter crash near Hue.

Defending the DMZ

I SURRENDER: A North Vietnamese Army trooper walks to the sweep line some 2,000m south of the DMZ to give himself up to Marines of the 1st Battalion, 9th Marines during Operation Prairie II in March 1967.

command. The Special Landing Force, now the 2d Battalion, 3d Marines, also arrived. These battalions had been issued the 5.56mm M-16 rifle in place of 7.62mm M-14s.

The decision to replace the M-14 with the M-16 had been made the previous year on Westmoreland's recommendation. Walt favored the Stoner system, which he had tested at Quantico but which was not in production. The M-16 was a favorite of McNamara's, it was being produced by Colt, and the

Marines could buy it from the Army for $121.00 a rifle. It proved at first a questionable weapon.

By 28 April the two battalions, with heavy air and artillery support, had taken Hill 861. In bitter fighting, Hill 881 South was taken on 2 May and Hill 881 North on 4 May.

On 8 May the North Vietnamese marked the 13th anniversary of the fall of Dien Bien Phu with particularly heavy bombardments of the northern camps. At Con Thien the barrage was followed by a futile assault by two battalions against the 1st Battalion, 4th Marines. Ten days later the Marines began Operation Hickory, a first-time entry in force into the lower half of the DMZ.

But on 22 May a letter from an unidentified Marine was read in the House of Representatives blaming the failure of the M-16 rifle for many Marine deaths in the fight for the Khe Sanh hills. The M-16, it was discovered, was not as forgiving as the M-14; the Marines lacked experience in its care, there was a shortage of cleaning gear, and the powder in the cartridges was not quite right. All these things were fixed by October and the M-16 became dependable, if unloved.

Big and burly Lieutenant General Walt, the personification of the Marines' war, was relieved on June as Commanding General, III Marine Amphibious Force, by equally big and burly Lieutenant General Robert E. Cushman, Jr. An outstanding battalion commander in World War II and with a Navy Cross for Guam, Cushman had also been for four years Vice President Nixon's Assistant for National Security Affairs. More recently he had commanded Camp Pendleton and the newly-activated 5th Marine Division.

Lt. Gen. Robert E. Cushman —took over command of the III Marine Amphibious Force from Lt. Gen. Walt in June 1967.

There were new enemy stirrings at Khe Sanh where the 26th Marines had relieved the 3d Marines. About 50 North Vietnamese attacked a radio relay station on Hill 950, five miles north of the airstrip. Next day, Company B of the 1st Battalion, 26th Marines, fought off two NVA companies a mile northwest of Hill 881 South. Cushman reinforced Khe Sanh's defenders with the 3d Battalion, 26th Marines. The enemy's probing actions trailed off and by mid-July seemed to be at an end.

Marine engineers had improved Route 9, now called 'Ryan's Road,' so that trucks could travel from Dong Ha to Khe Sanh. By the end of June they had also scraped a 'firebreak' 600 meters wide between Con Thien and Gio Linh as the first step in McNamara's barrier system.

During the summer the press had picked up on the clearing of the 'firebreak' south of the DMZ. In August the Senate Subcommittee on Preparedness held closed hearings on the barrier system. Wheeler, the Chairman of the JCS, gave a qualified endorsement. General Harold K. Johnson, Chief of Staff of

RIFLE QUIZ:
Maj. Gen. Herman Nickerson, Jr., asks one of the first Marines to receive the controversial new M-16 rifle for his opinion. Nearly 3.5 lbs. lighter than the M-14 it was to replace, the M-16 soon became the subject of a congressional debate. After the fighting in the Khe Sanh hills a letter from a Marine was read in Congress blaming the M-16 for many of the Marine deaths. Investigation showed a number of defects that were soon fixed. The M-16's reputation was later salvaged during the 1968 streetfighting in Hue where its ability to fire in automatic mode proved invaluable.

he Army, described it as "closing the window and eaving the door open." Marine Commandant Greene said flatly: "From the very beginning I have been opposed to this project."

McNamara did not take kindly to this dissent. He confirmed his decision to construct the barrier, barring any further public discussion by any member of the Department of Defense, military or civilian. The barrier was now dubbed 'McNamara's Wall' by the press. Rumors were just beginning to come out of Georgetown drawing rooms that McNamara was becoming disenchanted with the war.

The Marines fighting south of the DMZ had long since become disenchanted with Mr. McNamara. The press called Con Thien a "siege" and presented

Maj. Gen. Rathvon McC. Tompkins —shrewd tactician who took over command of the 3d Marine Division after the death of Gen. Hochmuth in November 1967.

Col. David E. Lownds —commanded the 26th Marines at Khe Sanh during early 1968. Later awarded the Navy Cross.

it as a "little Dien Bien Phu." Actually, th 158-meter-high hill, scraped down to raw red laterit by digging and shellfire, was never occupied by mor than a battalion and most fighting took place som distance away.

The closest the North Vietnamese got to the hil was a company-size probe. On 4 October, Westmore land announced that American firepower, includin a monumental effort by B-52s, had broken the bac of the month-long siege and the enemy had suffere a "crushing defeat."

The 3d Marine Division closed the books with th notation that 1,117 enemy had been killed and fiv prisoners taken compared to 340 Marines killec 3,086 wounded. In the Khe Sanh area enemy actio had been strangely light. In the whole summer, or ly 113 North Vietnamese had been killed at a cos to the 26th Marines of 10 dead, 39 wounded.

Vice President Hubert H. Humphrey visited th III Marine Amphibious Force on 1 November, fly ing in a four-engined transport within five miles the DMZ, close enough to see US artillery fire. Hun phrey received an optimistic briefing on III MA operations.

At a ceremony in Da Nang, Humphrey presente the Presidential Unit Citation to the 3d Marine Div sion for "extraordinary heroism in action" for th period 8 March 1965 to 15 September 1967. At n time during his visit did he mention that the facad of unity within the Johnson administration ha begun to crack or that McNamara had begun to hin at resignation.

General Hochmuth, the commander of the 3 Marine Division, was killed on 14 November whe his helicopter exploded and crashed northwest Hue. The new commander was Major Genera Rathvon McC. Tompkins, a shrewd tactician wh had received a Navy Cross as a battalion con mander at Saipan.

Khe Sanh had been almost quiet since the hil fights of April and May. Colonel David E. Lownds commanding the 26th Marines, and present himsel at Khe Sanh, had his 1st Battalion spread thin: company on Hill 881, another on Hill 861, a platoo on Hill 950, a company on the base perimeter an two platoons in reserve.

Westmoreland pressed the reluctant Cushman t

TRENCH WARFARE: For these two Marines sleeping with a ration box between them, the fighting at Con Thien was a business of fox holes, trench lines, mud, rain, and cold.

The press called the fighting around the Marine-occupied hill at Con Thien a siege and dubbed it a 'little Dien Bien Phu.' Eventually American fire power broke the enemy attack and ended the siege.

einforce Khe Sanh. Now that the monsoon rains ad come, Khe Sanh would have to be resupplied y air under very marginal flight conditions. ushman proposed he reinforce Khe Sanh modest-y and depend upon American air and ground irepower to destroy the enemy. Westmoreland greed.

On 13 December Cushman called Tompkins on the crambler phone, said he believed there were four nemy regiments in the vicinity of Khe Sanh, and uggested Tompkins add another battalion to its lefense. Tompkins moved the 3d Battalion, 26th Marines, to Khe Sanh and added a platoon of 105mm owitzers.

So 1967 ended with the uneasy expectation that omething big was about to happen.

Paddy Warfare

An Invisible Enemy

WHILE the battles against the North Vietnamese regulars were being fought along the DMZ, the more prosaic 'paddy war' against the Viet Cong continued.

Progress in pacifying the showcase Hoa Vang district south of Da Nang, despite the Ngu Hanh Son program so optimistically launched in October 1965, was disappointingly slow. US Marines were becoming increasingly aware of the truth of the old Vietnamese adage that the writ of the emperor did not extend past the village gate. They began to see the political-military structure of South Vietnam as a pyramid of war lords, in which, at the base, district chiefs hesitated to encroach on the prerogatives of village chiefs and sometimes reached accommodations with the Viet Cong, where the optimism of province chiefs did not square with reality, where corps commanders hesitated to give categoric orders to division commanders, and where the president and premier were rivals for power.

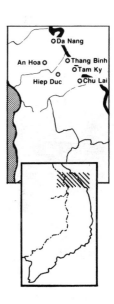

The government cadre placed in the five villages south of Da Nang was undertrained and no match for the Viet Cong effort to make the program fail. Groping for ways to get things moving, the 9th Marines introduced a new technique, 'County Fair,' in February 1966 to break down the Viet Cong 'infrastructure,' the cells of five to ten guerrillas buried deep in virtually every hamlet. The procedure was to ring the target hamlet during darkness and at dawn inform the inhabitants the hamlet was to be searched. All villagers were moved into an assembly area where a census was taken and identity cards were checked. A temporary dispensary was set up. Food and refreshments were passed out. Entertainment was provided—movies sometimes, or live entertainers, or a Marine Corps band or drum and bugle corps. Meanwhile the hamlet was being given a thorough going-over by Vietnamese soldiers and officials. Almost always something was found: propaganda, arms caches, sometimes Viet Cong. This was nothing more than an elaborated cordon-and search operation—but it worked.

County Fairs and other counterguerrilla operations in Quang Nam were best with the active involvement of the ARVN 51st Regiment. This, of course, was on the basis of cooperation. Later the colonel of the 9th Marines compared operating with the 51st Regiment as attempting to play soccer and football on the same field on the same Sunday afternoon.

General Kyle, after taking over the 3d Marine Division in March 1966, systematized things more with a series of operations designed to scrub clean the area from Da Nang south to Hoi An.

'Kings' moved the forward edge of the 9th Marines to Route 4. 'Georgia' put a battalion of the regiment into An Hoa, an embryonic hydroelectric and chemical complex 20 air miles southeast of Da Nang. 'Liberty' broadened the front, bringing the 3d Marines in on the 9th Marines' right flank and the 1st Marines in on the left. The pacification which was to progress behind this shield was disastrously disrupted by the Buddhist Revolt during which the ARVN 51st Regiment literally walked off the battlefield. However, by the 4th of July the road was open from Da Nang south to Dai Loc on Route 4 and by the end of August from Dai Loc south to An Hoa.

The chief interference came from the remarkable Doc Lap Battalion, a Viet Cong Main Force unit masters at mining, ambushes, and sharp sudden attacks against units of up to company size. Operation Macon was launched to finish the Doc Lap Battalion. Macon lasted three months and involved as many as five Marine battalions. Some 507 dead Viet Cong were counted, but Doc Lap survived.

More Marine battalions were needed. The Marine Corps had a well-trained 4th Marine Division and 4th Marine Aircraft Wing in the Organized Reserve but Johnson and McNamara had decided that Vietnam would be fought without calling up the Reserve. Some individuals would volunteer for active service but the units would sit out the war. However, the Services were authorized to increase the size of

PFC James Anderson, Jr. —received the Congressional Medal of Honor posthumously for bravery while serving as a rifleman at Cam Lo in February 1967.

regular establishments. The 5th Marine Division was formed at Camp Pendleton in California. The first unit activated was Regimental Landing Team 26—the 26th Marines with accompanying slices of division troops, including a battalion of the 13th Marines, the 5th Division's artillery regiment. Activation of the 27th and 28th Marines followed.

In the September election, Thieu was elected to a four-year term as president and Ky out-maneuvered from premier to the less powerful position of vice president. Charges of irregularities in the balloting were brushed aside. The election to choose members of the Constituent Assembly took place on 11 September. Some 80 per cent of the 5,288,512 registered voters turned out, heralded as a clear-cut endorsement of the Thieu-Ky government.

In October, the 1st Marine Division, commanded by Major General Herman Nickerson, Jr., moved headquarters north from Chu Lai to the bunkered command post vacated by the 3d Marine Division on Hill 327 outside of Da Nang. Task Force X-Ray, with two battalions, was left at Chu Lai.

The 2d Korean Marine Corps 'Blue Dragon' Brigade had come into Quang Ngai province. The 1st Marine Aircraft Wing, now under Major General Louis B. Robertshaw, a squadron commander at Guadalcanal, was operating from five fields. Helicopter groups MAG-16 and MAG-36 were at Marble Mountain near Da Nang and Ky Ha at Chu Lai. A helicopter squadron was at Phu Bai. One fixed-wing group, MAG-11, was at Da Nang; two others, MAG-12 and MAG-13, at Chu Lai.

The Western year 1967 began with a New Year's truce—48 hours of uneasy, distrustful stand-down. It was followed by *Tet,* the lunar New Year, from 8 to 12 February, and its much-violated promises of a ceasefire.

On 27 February Soviet-manufactured 140mm spin-stabilized rockets were used against Da Nang air base for the first time. About 50 of the erratic rockets were gotten off. Although electronically detonated, the launcher was not much more than a tube fastened to a board in a shallow pit. Fourteen Air Force and three Marine aircraft were damaged, ten Americans were killed and 26 more wounded, but most of the destruction was to nearby Ap Do hamlet, where 32 civilians were killed.

Bell UH-1E— better known as the 'Huey.' Although capable of lifting up to 4,000 lbs. of cargo or eight passengers, Hueys were mainly used by the Marines for observation and liaison. Marine doctrine called for employment in pairs—one unarmed "slick" and one "gunship" equipped with machine gun and rocket pods.

THE ONTOS
(from the
Greek for
the 'thing')

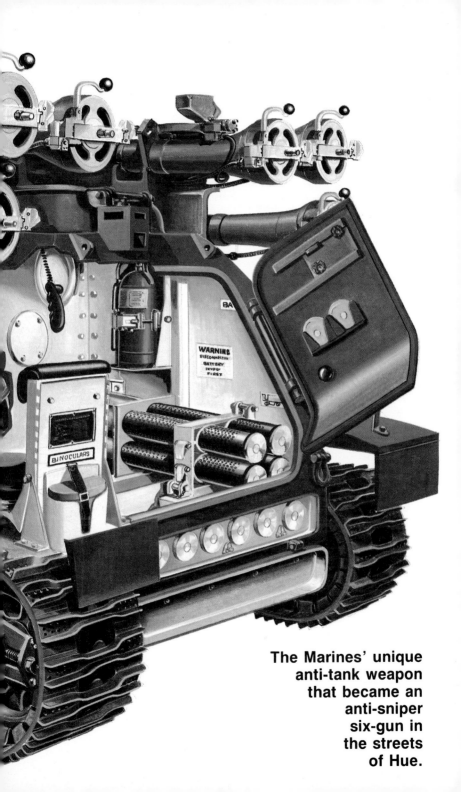

The Marines' unique
anti-tank weapon
that became an
anti-sniper
six-gun in
the streets
of Hue.

During search operations Marines would cordon a village at dawn and systematically search every inch including underground bunkers for Viet Cong, arms caches, and enemy propaganda leaflets.

Westmoreland had promised Army troops for the southern two provinces. The 196th Light Infantry Brigade with four battalions arrived at Chu Lai. Task Force Oregon, a headquarters for all Army units, was set up under command of Major General William B Rosson, Westmoreland's former chief of staff. Then the 3d Brigade, 25th Division, arrived and on 26 April Rosson assumed responsibility for the Chu Lai TAOR. With Army troops in place, the 7th Marines moved north to Da Nang and the 9th Marines to Dong Ha.

Paddy Warfare

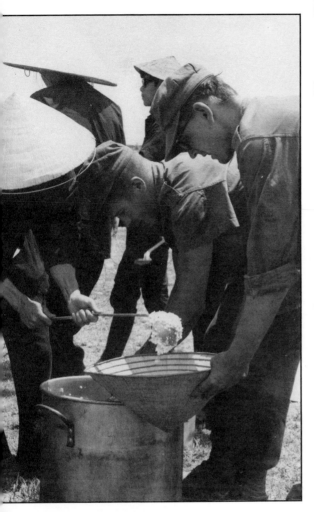

HEARTS & STOMACHS: County Fair search and cordon operations were refined into hard and soft plays. The Vietnamese forces would conduct the searches while the Marines would keep the hamlet inhabitants occupied with free food and entertainment. To the S.Vietnamese used to a rice diet these hand-outs of flour and ham were a new experience.

On 21 April a company from the 2d Battalion, 1st Marines, coming south from Da Nang, ran into a dug-in Viet Cong battalion just west of Thang Binh. What followed was almost a repeat of the old Harvest Moon battle 18 months earlier: Two Marine battalions helicoptered into the valley and swept back to the northeast, while the ARVN 1st Ranger Group with three battalions drove southwestward.

The climax came in mid-May with a two-battalion fight for Hill 110. The operation 'Union,' ended with the extraordinary claim of 865 enemy killed, 777

THE AMTRAC

Otherwise known as an amphibian tractor and officially designated as an LVTP-5, (Landing Vehicle, Tracked, Personnel).

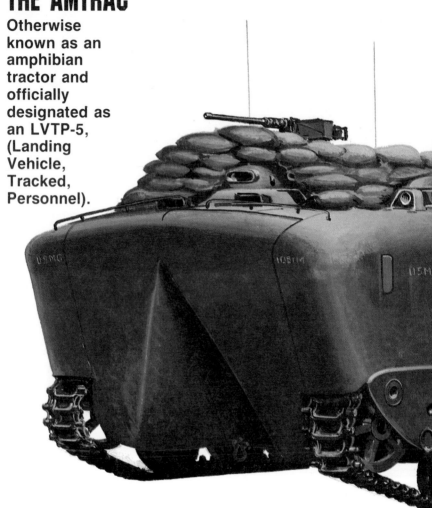

Although originally intended to transport Marines to assault beaches the 'amtrac' was used principally in Vietnam as a troop transport capable of carrying up to 34 combat-loaded Marines across inland waterways. Its standard armament, a .30 cal. machine gun, inside the rear-mounted turret had a limited field of fire on land. Extra firepower was added with an M-60 machine gun laid across sandbags at the front of the amtrac.

Sgt. Rodney M. Davis —received a posthumous Medal of Honor for his gallantry while serving in Quang Nam province.

'probables,' and 173 prisoners. Two fresh enemy regiments, the NVA 3d and 21st, were reported in the valley. Union II, fought in concert with the ARVN 6th Regiment and the ARVN 1st Ranger Group, began with a Marine battalion landing some 19 miles northwest of Tam Ky. They found the North Vietnamese main body in well-fortified positions on the southern rim. Union II lasted 11 bloody days and the Marines entered 540 more enemy dead onto the gruesome scorecard. Marine losses for both Union I and II were a stiff 220 killed and 714 wounded.

On 15 June two enemy companies surfaced just four miles south of Thang Binh. A third round of fighting went on until the beginning of July.

The enemy, for the first time using 122mm rockets—lighter, longer-ranged, and more accurate than the 140mms—south of the DMZ, landed 50 on Da Nang air base after midnight on 15 July, destroying two Marine F-8E Crusaders and damaging a third; 37 Marines were wounded. The Air Force lost two C-130s and six F-4Cs, and had eight airmen killed and 138 wounded. The launchers were found in Hoa Hung village, six miles southwest.

In August, the 1st Marines moved through the densely populated area east of Highway One and south of Hoi An, counting 100 enemy killed against eight Marines dead and 60 wounded. A little further to the south, the 5th Marines went once again into the much-fought-over Thang Binh-Tam Ky-Hiep Duc triangle, repeating the Harvest Moon and Union operations. 'Cochise,' also with the cooperation of the ARVN 2d Division, provided an impressive body count. The Marines claimed 156 killed and 13 captured, with losses being ten killed and 81 wounded.

There was more fighting in Que Son valley in September. Two Marine battalions converged on an enemy battalion near Hill 63. The battle built up, Task Force X-Ray was reactivated to take command, and fighting went on until 15 September.

Final count was 571 enemy dead, eight prisoners. American losses were 127 dead, 362 wounded. The NVA 2d Division was buffeted back and forth, east and west, north and south, but never destroyed—always disappearing back into the mountains to rebuild its strength. There seemed also to be no way

to stop the stand-off attacks against the airfields. Marble Mountain was hit with 140mm rockets on 28 August. Three helicopters were destroyed and 20 damaged along with five Marines dead and 54 wounded. (The infantry Marines always cocked a skeptical eyebrow at the large number of wounded in the rocket attacks: Few wounded were hospitalized, but all certified for Purple Hearts.)

On 22 September, Task Force Oregon became the American or 23d Division, picking up the name and number of a division that had fought by the side of the Marines at Guadalcanal. (It had gotten its peculiar name 'American' because it was first formed on New Caledonia in 1942.)

On 28 September the *New York Times* reported that two-thirds of the Marines' transport helicopters

AMTRAC: **Marine amtracs —amphibian tractors—were originally designed for ship-to-shore movement. In Vietnam amtracs were frequently used as substitutes for armored personnel carriers.**

Paddy Warfare

BEFORE THE SIEGE: Marines of the 2d Bn., 3d Marines , lead an attack on Hill 881 N at Khe Sanh in April 1967. Denial of these outlying hills above the combat base would later prove a crucial if costly tactic in the 77-day siege that was to come.

were grounded because "their tail assemblies were falling apart." The Boeing-built CH-46As and CH-46Ds had been rushed into South Vietnam beginning in April 1966 to replace the venerable Sikorsky UH-34Ds. Eight had crashed in Southeast Asia and four more in the United States. A modification program was completed in December 1967.

That month the 11th Infantry Brigade joined the Americal Division, freeing the Korean Marine 'Blue Dragon' Brigade to move north from Chu Lai to a TAOR south of Da Nang and west of Hoi An.

Opposition to the war in the press and in Congress was growing. In November, Johnson summoned Westmoreland to Washington to rally support for the war.

He made a televised address at the National Press Club, predicting that the withdrawal of US forces could begin within two years. To most viewers it sounded as though he were saying the war was won. A week later it was announced that Secretary of Defense Robert S. McNamara was to become president of the World Bank.

Tet Offensive

6

The Battle for Hue

ON the second day of the New Year, a Marine platoon patrolling out of Khe Sanh encountered a North Vietnamese reconnaissance party, and killed five—including a regimental commander. Westmoreland took this as clinching evidence that the long-expected NVA offensive was about to begin.

Returns showed that 81,249 of 298,498 Marines were in Vietnam, including 21 of the 36 infantry battalions, 14 of 33 fixed-wing squadrons, and 13 of 24 helicopter squadrons. No other US service yielded such a high proportion.

The Army's Americal Division was in Quang Ngai and Quang Tin provinces. The Marine air and all American ground troops, equivalent to a field army, were under Cushman's operational command.

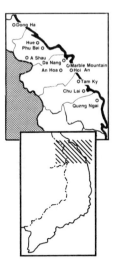

Because of political sensitivities, Cushman had something called 'operational guidance' rather than command over the 'Blue Dragon' Brigade's 6,000 superbly conditioned troops. Between Cushman and General Lam there were no command lines. General Lam commanded 80,000 South Vietnamese—ARVN regulars, Regional Forces, and Popular Forces. There were 73 Free World infantry battalions—close to a quarter-million men under arms in I Corps.

"During January," Westmoreland later wrote, "we began to receive numerous reports about a major offensive to be undertaken just before or during *Tet*."

He put his staff to work planning a massive aerial counteroffensive, Operation Niagara. He also asked for a historical analysis of Dien Bien Phu—Westmoreland was a man with a sense of destiny. The chess pieces were being arranged for the decisive battle. As a further reinforcement of the north, Westmoreland ordered the 1st Air Cavalry

Tet Offensive

SANDBAG CITY: As the fighting against NVA regulars intensified south of the DMZ, Marine defensive positions looked increasingly like the trenchlines and bunkers of World War I. This position near Cam Lo had just survived a three-hour shelling. One of the first Marines to emerge checks a fuel drum for shellfire damage.

Division and the 2d Brigade, 101st Airborne Division, into Quang Tri and Thua Thien.

By mid-January Westmoreland's J-2 told him that the NVA 304th Division had crossed the border from Laos and joined the 325C Division outside Khe Sanh. A deserter said that some of the 308th and 341st Divisions were also south of the DMZ. To the east of Khe Sanh the 320th Division seemed poised to attack Camp Carroll and the Rockpile.

Cushman continued to disagree with Westmore-

and on the importance of Khe Sanh. Very conscious
of the monsoon which was now blowing and that the
continued resupply by air would have to be done
under marginal flight conditions, he proposed to
reinforce the base modestly and depend upon air and
ground firepower to destroy the enemy. Westmoreland agreed.

General Tompkins, his responsibility for Thua
Thien relieved by the arrival of Task Force X-Ray,
moved his 3d Marine Division command post

Over 100,000 civilians were caught in the cross-fire of the fighting in Hue. Persuading civilians to leave their homes was not always easy.

forward from Phu Bai to Dong Ha. SLF Bravo had been working north and south of the Cua Viet estuary. SLF Alpha landed in Thua Thien province near Camp Evans, which was being prepared for the 1st Air Cavalry Division. Tompkins moved the 2d Battalion, 26th Marines, from Phu Bai to Khe Sanh. This gave Lownds all three of his organic battalions.

Lownds had most of his infantry strength up in the hills. On 20 January one company ran into a North Vietnamese battalion in the saddle between Hills 881 South and 881 North. The company fell back to join another company on Hill 881 S, which the North Vietnamese then surrounded, but failed to take. That night the company on Hill 861 beat off an attack and at dawn a torrent of 122mm rockets fell on the main base. Khe Sanh lost its main ammo dump and much of its fuel. Cushman gave Lownds the 1st Battalion, 9th Marines, which was put in about a mile southwest of the base.

Westmoreland put Operation Niagara into effect. Marine, Air Force, and Navy tactical air ringed Khe Sanh, while at a greater range Strategic Air Command's B-52s carpeted the hills with bombs. The NVA 66th Regiment, 304th Division, drove the Laotian 33d Battalion across the border into the CIDG camp at Lang Vei, seven miles from Khe Sanh.

It was politically desirable to get some South Vietnamese into the fight. The lightly armed 37th Rangers, with a strength of only 318, arrived and were given a sector on the east of the perimeter. Two more batteries of 105mm howitzers came in. This gave Lownds five infantry battalions and a reinforced artillery battalion. The base also fell within the range fan of the eighteen 175mm guns of the Army's 2d Battalion, 94th Artillery, at Camp Carroll and the Rockpile.

The Viet Cong announced a country-wide *Tet* truce from 27 January until 3 February. The South Vietnamese countered with a 36-hour cease-fire beginning on 29 January. No one expected either to hold.

Viet Cong activity in Quang Nam centered on the triangle formed by Da Nang and Hoi An on the coast and, inland, An Hoa, now developed into a major Marine combat base. In addition to the Doc Lap Battalion, the presence of the NVA 368B Artillery Regiment had been confirmed. The rockets that came showering down on Marine installations were erratic but deadly.

The 1st Marine Division had five battalions in Quang Nam. West and southwest of Da Nang was the 7th Marines. South, between Highway One and the sea, were the 3d Battalion, 5th Marines, and the 2d Battalion, 3d Marines.

The enemy *Tet* offensive began in I Corps on 29 January with rocket and mortar attacks against Da Nang and Marble Mountain air bases. The following night Marble Mountain and Chu Lai were shelled.

The enemy's apparent strategy was to freeze the Americans in base areas, while attacking provincial and district capitals. On 30 and 31 January the ARVN, with US Army help, repulsed attacks against Tam Ky in Quang Tin province. Much the same happened at Quang Ngai.

To the north, two NVA battalions got into Quang Tri city, but units of the ARVN 1st Division, with US Army help, drove them out. The enemy's main effort was reserved for Da Nang and Hue.

At Da Nang the enemy had infiltrated close to Lam's headquarters east of the air base. The attack against the I Corps headquarters, behind a screen of mortar shells and rockets, was beaten off by South Vietnamese military police, Rangers, and US Marine military police.

Apparently this was meant to be a disruption to cover a large-scale move against Da Nang. Marine reconnaissance detected sizable forces in the blue-green foothills of the Annamites west of An Hoa. These were brought under heavy air attack and artillery fire. The 3d Battalion, 5th Marines, rescued two Regional Force companies nearly engulfed at the hamlet of Thon Trung Luong.

Two regiments of North Vietnamese regulars had infiltrated into Hue to join local Viet Cong. After midnight on 31 January they seized most of the ancient imperial capital.

Hue was South Vietnam's third largest city. Two-thirds of its nominal population of 100,000 (and uncounted number of refugees) lived inside the massive walls of the Old City. The southeast wall ran along the Song Huong, or River of Perfumes. The New City was south of the river. Until now both sides had treated Hue as something of an open city. There was

AH-1 Huey Cobra —both the Army and the Marines had demonstrated the need for a fast heavily-armed helicopter. The two-seater Huey Cobra was the result of a crash program to meet that need. These early models carried a center-mounted minigun 7.62mm machine gun capable of firing 8,000 rounds. Mounted on each of the stub wings are 76 2.5-inch rockets.

Tet Offensive

ROCKET ROUND: On a hilltop south of Khe Sanh, Marines from 1st Battalion, 4th Marines watch for the effect of a round fired from a 66mm M-72 disposable rocket launcher.

no US military garrison. Task Force X-Ray, headquartered at Phu Bai eight miles to the south, was not detailed to defend Hue. Brigadier General Foster Lahue, with three under-strength battalions, was supposed to keep Highway One open from Hai Van pass north to Hue, defend the western approaches to the capital, and defend the base at Phu Bai.

A group of Army and Marine advisors were in a compound in the New City at a considerable distance from the headquarters of the ARVN 1st Division in

the northeastern corner of the Old City. General
Truong had the 12 battalions strung out along
Highway One from Hue north to the border, but in
Hue only his headquarters and the elite 'Black Pan-
ther' Company. By daylight the North Vietnamese
flag was flying over the Imperial Palace and the
North Vietnamese held all of the Old City except
Truong's compound.

At Phu Bai, Lahue, knowing very little of what
was going on in Hue, sent out a company on a

motorized reconnaissance. It was stopped halfway to the city. Lahue then dispatched the 1st Battalion, 1st Marines, command group and a second company. The two-company force broke through to the MACV compound and was ordered to cross the Nguyen Hoang bridge into the Old City and proceed to Truong's headquarters. The Marines got across the bridge but without support fell back to the MACV compound.

The ARVN 3d Regiment and two Airborne battalions fought down from the north and reached Truong, who then counterattacked toward the Imperial Palace.

General Lam asked General Cushman if the Americans would take over completely the clearing of the New City. Although the situation was not as catastrophic as first appeared, pockets of Regional Force and Popular Force units still held out.

ARVN's General Lam —requested the Marines to clear the New City of Hue.

The 1st Battalion, 1st Marines, attacked toward the provincial headquarters but failed to retake it. The 2d Battalion, 5th Marines, with two companies, was fed into the fight and Colonel Stanley S. Hughes of the 1st Marines took command.

More Marine rifle companies arrived to flesh out the two battalions and the counterattack began in earnest on 4 February. The Viet Cong and North Vietnamese had hurriedly fortified the governmental buildings into strong points so the Marines battered their way in with tanks and assault guns.

In the Old City, Truong's counterattack bogged down. He was reinforced with two battalions of Vietnamese Marines and the 1st Battalion, 5th Marines. Because the Old City was a rabbit warren, the fighting was essentially house-to-house. On 23 February Truong made a final assault against the Imperial Palace. At dawn the red-barred yellow flag of South Vietnam flew once more over the Citadel.

The battle for Hue had cost Truong 357 killed, 1,830 wounded, and 42 missing. He claimed 2,642 enemy dead and 33 prisoners. The US Marines had lost 142 killed and 857 seriously wounded, and claimed 1,959 enemy killed and 12 prisoners taken. Some 2,800 civilians, killed by communist death squads, were found in mass graves. Another 3,000 were missing, the majority presumed dead.

At Khe Sanh on 5 February, the North Vietnamese again failed to capture Hill 861. The follow-

ing night, mortar and artillery shells thundered down on Khe Sanh and Lang Vei. The NVA 66th Regiment crashed into the Lang Vei camp behind a dozen Soviet-built PT-76 amphibian tanks. Only about half the 500 defenders, covered by air strikes, escaped. By the end of the day Lang Vei was empty and 3,000-5,000 refugees were at the barbed wire gates of Khe Sanh. Lownds would not let them in until screened by the Green Berets. Then they were evacuated by air to Cam Lo.

Westmoreland arrived in a cold fury at Cushman's headquarters at Da Nang. As he saw it, the Marines, having failed to reinforce Lang Vei, then failed to rescue its defenders.

Westmoreland was also disturbed by the failure of the Marines to provide tactical air support for the 1st Cavalry Division.

Westmoreland had already decided to open a MACV forward command post in I Corps. His deputy ground commander, General Creighton W. Abrams, took up residence at Phu Bai. The headquarters of the 1st Air Cavalry Division was already there, planning the airmobile relief of Khe Sanh.

It was feverishly reported in the media, mostly by journalists who got no closer to Khe Sanh than

ARMORED AMTRAC: An amphibian tractor with a 105mm howitzer fires a mission in support of a 1st Marine Division action in Quang Nam province. Armed with 105s, they had good mobility in the sands and rice paddies of ICTZ but were too thinly armored to be used as tanks.

Tet Offensive

STREETFIGHTERS: Battle-weary Marines of Company D, 1st Battalion, 5th Marines advance in loose column through the devastated Old City of Hue on 24 February, 1968, after recapturing the Citadel and bringing the month-long battle to an end.

The 1/5 saw the worst of the fighting. Stationed in the Old City, they fought house-to-house against VC and NVA units who had been ordered to stay until the bitter end.

The Marines suffered the loss of 142 lives in Hue.

ELEPHANT GRASS: Much of the area south of the DMZ was covered by seven-foot-high elephant grass. It severely limited patrols and foot movement and provided the enemy with an ideal hiding place. Defoliant and napalm were used to destroy it wherever possible.

Saigon, that the North Vietnamese had mounted a classic siege, complete with trenches, zig-zags, and parallels. There were rumors of mining and tunneling under the American lines. Actually, the North Vietnamese were being held at arm's length from Khe Sanh. The airstrip and main base got the heavier part of the shelling but most of the infantry action was out in the hills.

All resupply and reinforcements came in by air, at first by C-123 Providers and C-130 Hercules to the strip and then up into the hills by helicopter. By mid-February the transports were dropping loads by parachute or having them snatched out of rear cargo doors by a drag parachute or an arresting line. By the month's end the Marines had used up half the CH-46 helicopters of HMM-262 and another medium transport squadron, HMM-364, had to help. Helicopter loads now came from Dong Ha, 20 miles away.

Reaction in Washington to the *Tet* offensive

brought a fresh wave of troops to South Vietnam. First units of RLT-27, taken from the 5th Marine Division at Camp Pendleton, arrived at Da Nang on 17 February. The new regiment moved into the still-troublesome area south from Marble Mountain to Hoi An, permitting the remainder of the 5th Marines to go north of Hai Van pass.

The shelling of Khe Sanh peaked in the last week of February. On the last night of the month a battalion of 304th Division got as far as the sector held by the 37th Rangers. Tompkins visited the base almost daily, a dangerous bit of personal leadership. Cushman remained imperturbable. It was Tompkins' and Lownds' fight and he was satisfied with their tactics.

Westmoreland found Cushman's phlegm irritating. More and more dissatisfied with Marine Corps generalship, he introduced a new layer of tactical command between Cushman and his northern divisions. He replaced his advance command post at Phu Bai with a new headquarters, Provisional Corps, Vietnam, under Rosson, now a lieutenant general. Rosson's new corps included the 3d Marine Division, the 101st Airborne and 1st Air Cavalry Divisions. Rosson's deputy was Marine Major General Raymond Davis, who, as a battalion commander, had a Navy Cross for Peleliu in World War II and a Medal of Honor for the Chosin Reservoir in Korea.

But the battle for Khe Sanh was almost over. The 325C Division was already withdrawing and Cushman ordered Lownds to extend patrolling. Operation Pegasus, the long-planned airmobile relief, began, as planned, on 1 April. The 'flying horses' of the 1st Air Cavalry Division leap-frogged forward while the 1st Marines and three ARVN battalions advanced more mundanely along Route 9. On 6 April, Westmoreland, back in Washington, announced the arrival of the Air Cavalry at Khe Sanh in a press conference on the White House lawn.

The 'relief' caused no wild rejoicing at Khe Sanh. The Marines had never felt any imminent danger of being overrun, but there was still hard fighting ahead. Rearguard North Vietnamese estimated at a battalion strength clung stubbornly to Hill 881 North. The Marines sallied forth from Hill 881 South on Easter morning and took the hill. Next day Pegasus officially ended. The Marines had lost a

PFC Ralph H. Johnson —posthumous recipient of the Medal of Honor for gallantry while serving as a reconnaisance scout in the Quan Duc Duc valley in March 1968.

Tet Offensive

EAR SHATTERING:
A shell in flight fired from a 'howtar,' a 4.2-inch mortar. Mounted on the carriage of a 75mm pack howitzer, it was a uniquely Marine weapon. The 4.2-inch was the largest of the Marine mortars, with an effective range of 4,000m.

total of 199 men killed and 830 seriously wounded from the beginning of the battle to the end of March. Pegasus had cost another 92 Marines and soldiers killed and 629 seriously wounded. The Marines had counted about 1,000 North Vietnamese dead. Westmoreland's staff put the total North Vietnamese loss at from 10,000 to 15,000.

Johnson nominated McNamara's replacement as Secretary of Defense on 19 January. He was handsome 62-year-old Clark McAdams Clifford, veteran Washington lawyer and Democratic politician with a reputation as a troubleshooter. The Senate confirmed him unanimously and on 1 March Clifford took his place in Room 3E880 in the Pentagon behind the massive walnut desk that had once served General of the Armies John J. Pershing. It was a cream-smooth transition, partly because of Clifford's personality and partly because it was understood that it was an interim arrangement until the 1969 inauguration.

Capt. James E. Livingston —received the Medal of Honor for bravery while serving as the commanding officer of Co. E, 2d Battalion, 4th Marines at Dai Do in May 1968.

Then President Johnson stunned the nation on 31 March with a televised announcement that he was de-escalating the war, reducing the bombing of the North, initiating preliminary peace talks, and that he had decided not to seek re-election. On 10 April he announced that Abrams would replace Westmoreland in July. This was no surprise. Cushman recommended that Khe Sanh be abandoned, saying that the western approaches into Quang Tri province could be covered better by mobile operations. Westmoreland agreed but said that the final decision should be Abrams'. Both Cushman and Rosson argued for the dismantling of the ineffective and never-completed McNamara Wall, which had tied up so much of the 3d Marine Division's resources. Westmoreland again deferred to Abrams. Cushman now turned his attention to a good-weather spring counteroffensive, beginning with a raid by the 1st Air Cavalry and 101st Airborne Divisions against the enemy's base area in A Shau valley, much-used to support operations against Hue. Davis attached himself to the Air Cavalry for this raid and was impressed by the Army's bold use of helicopters.

Cushman also planned a cleansing attack into the DMZ. Before this could take place the NVA 320th Division came down in an attack aimed at the 3d Marine Division headquarters at Dong Ha. A six-

A Marine prepares to fire a 60mm mortar. This smooth-bore muzzle-loaded weapon was the smallest of the mortars used by the Marines. The "sixty" was regarded fondly by the artillery companies as their "organic" artillery. Barrel, bipods and baseplate altogether weighed only 45 lbs. Its effective range, with the improved high explosive shell, was about 1900 meters.

day battle centering on the hamlet of Dai Do, barely outside Dong Ha, began. Heavy fighting continued until the end of May, when the 320th withdrew once again to its sanctuary. By this time Davis had relieved Tompkins as commander of the 3d Marine Division.

Otherwise, May was characterized in I Corps by 'mini-Tet,' mostly wide-ranging mortar and rocket attacks but including a serious effort to take Tam Ky.

Allen Brook, a sizable operation against the NVA 36th Regiment, was mounted in May, first under the 7th Marines, and then, when the 7th Marines swung north of An Hoa to comb the corridors leading down from the mountains toward Da Nang, under the 27th Marines.

In the north the NVA 304th Division had come back into western Quang Tin province and there was sharp fighting radiating out from Khe Sanh. By the end of May two regiments of the NVA 308th Division were found south of Khe Sanh. Davis went after the two regiments using Task Force Hotel, to which was assigned the 1st and 4th Marines, in a high-mobility operation using landing zones and fire support bases blasted through the rain forest canopy. Robin North (1st Marines) and Robin South (4th Marines) went on for three weeks in June and cost the North Vietnamese 725 dead and captured, and large amounts of material. The NVA 308th Division, rendered ineffective, withdrew north to rebuild.

On 1 June, General Krulak was relieved as Commanding General, Fleet Marine Force, Pacific, by Lieutenant General Henry W. Buse, Jr., ending 34 years of active service for the brilliant, controversial 'Brute' Krulak. Westmoreland, returning to Washington to be Chief of Staff of the Army, held a last press conference on 10 June. He was asked if the war could be won militarily. "Not in the classic sense, because—" Westmoreland paused briefly, "—of our national policy of not expanding the war."

The next day Abrams authorized the evacuation of Khe Sanh. On 1 August Major General Richard G. Stilwell, USA, relieved Rosson as Commanding General, Provisional Corps, Vietnam, and two weeks later the Provisional Corps became the XXIV Corps.

Fighting in Quang Nam through the summer centered on the Allen Brook operations around Go

Noi island and the Mameluke Thrust operations around An Hoa. The 5th Marines had returned from above the Hai Van pass and had moved into An Hoa, taking over this area from the 7th Marines. Despite these spoiling operations the North Vietnamese once again managed to get an attack force within striking distance of Da Nang.

As the month ended, the 1st Marines returned from the north to rejoin its parent 1st Marine Division, being given the old familiar battleground to the south of Da Nang between the highway and the sea. The 27th Marines, borrowed from the 5th Marine Division, departed for Camp Pendleton.

In the north the 3d Marine Division was once more fighting its old enemy, the NVA 320th Division. In a two-pronged attack launched from the Rockpile, the 9th Marines, now commanded by Colonel Robert H. Barrow, went against the Nui Tia Pong ridge, west of the Rockpile, and then swung north against Dong Tien mountain, securing it on 9 September. The 3d Marines moved north of the Rockpile to Mutter's Ridge and then west against Hill 461, taking it on 11 September.

October brought monsoon rains with as much as 12-15 inches falling on Dong Ha and Da Nang a day. On 31 October President Johnson announced to the world that he was halting all air, naval, and artillery bombardment of North Vietnam. The Paris peace talks were about to begin.

In Washington, the Johnson administration was nearing the end. President-elect Richard M. Nixon announced that Congressman Melvin R. Laird would be his Secretary of Defense. In his campaigning, Nixon had promised a "secret" plan for ending the war.

TANK COUNTRY: A Marine M-48 sits semi-camouflaged waiting for any sign of the Viet Cong during Operation Kentucky, near Con Thien in February 1968. The Marines tanks were more useful in the relatively dry and open piedmont country in the north than in the rice paddies of the south or the mountains to the west.

Standing Down

The Beginning of the End

BY 1969 the Marine base camps had grown into fortified garrison towns. Inside the barbed wire life was comfortable, threatened only by occasional rockets and mortars.

Airy screened 'Southeast Asia' huts had replaced dank and suffocating tentage. Macadam covered much of the red mud. There were post exchanges, chapels, clubs stratified by rank, and plentiful electricity for radios, televisions, refrigeration, and even air conditioning. Food was good.

By a budgeting peculiarity, Marines got a third larger ration allowance than the Army. This translated into steaks, sometimes lobster, and for those on watch or coming back from patrol a fourth meal at midnight. A dairy had been built in the support area in Da Nang, a marvel of pipes and stainless steel where milk was reconstituted and turned into cottage cheese, ice cream, and milk shakes. Even for Marines on outposts or fire support bases food could be good, helicoptered in picnic-style.

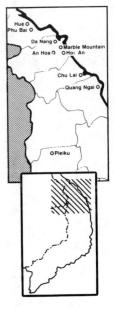

Mid-way through his year-long Vietnam tour a Marine could expect a six-day 'rest-and-recreation' leave that would take him at no cost to a place of his choice, to Hawaii if he had a wife to meet or, if he were footloose, as most were, Tokyo, Hong Kong, Sydney, Bangkok, or Taipei.

But there was a darker side. Officers and senior NCOs were coming back for a second tour. They saw a sameness to the war and things they did not like. Drugs were cheap and plentiful and more and more Marines were using them. There was racial strife, unknown in 1965, below the surface. Black Marines more and more stayed apart from white Marines, played their own music on their stereo tape decks, Japanese-made and bought remarkably cheap from

81'S IN ACTION: A round is dropped into an 81mm mortar with a 4000m range.

the post exchange, wore Black Power symbols, and had a half-secret organization, the 'Mau Maus.'

There were more accidental shootings than there should have been and some 'fraggings,' called so because the usual weapon was a grenade used against a sleeping officer or NCO. An anxious Marine Corps concluded that the roots were not racial but a rub-off of what was happening back in

The World, as the Marines sardonically called the States, where the campuses were aflame and demonstrators by the tens of thousands marched on The Mall in Washington or stormed the steps of the Pentagon.

The altruism of 1965 had worn thin. Few senior officers still saw the war as a crusade against communism. It was a job to be done and at the tactical level it was being done quite efficiently. Fire support bases by now were being widely used by both the 1st and 3d Marine Divisions, particularly in the western mountains. Special bombs blasted a hole through the double or triple canopy to clear a helo landing zone on top of a ridge or mountain. Then engineers came in with mini-dozers and demolitions. A typical FSB would have a composite battery of artillery (105mm and 155mm howitzers and 4.2-inch mortars), an infantry battalion command post, a logistic support area, and an aid station. Well-wrapped with barbed wire and antipersonnel mines, they were easily defended by a small force.

On 22 January General Davis sent the 9th Marines under Colonel Barrow into the valley in Operation Dewey Canyon, a high-mobility operation completely dependent upon helicopters. Three fire support bases, Shiloh, Razor, and Cunningham, were developed with others opening as the regiment moved forward. The heaviest fighting involved the 1st Battalion, 9th Marines, in the center of the line. By 19 March Da Krong valley seemed cleaned out, 1,617 enemy dead had been counted and a huge amount of material taken, including 1,461 weapons and hundreds of tons of ammunition and other supplies. Rated the most successful regimental operation of the war, the cost to the Marines was 121 dead and 611 wounded. Barrow, as a lieutenant in World War II, had served with Chinese guerrillas behind the Japanese lines, and, as a captain, had commanded a rifle company in Korea. He would go on to become Commandant of the Marine Corps in 1979.

The ritual of a *Tet* truce was again announced, 24 hours of suspended operations beginning on 16 February, and was observed with the usual violations: rocket and mortar attacks, assassinations, and scattered ground action.

An attack once again came up from the south and out of the west against Da Nang. The two highway bridges over the Song Cau Do in Hoa Vang district below the airfield were briefly threatened and some Viet Cong and NVA units surfaced in the city. Sappers tried to get to the 1st Marine Division headquarters on Hill 327 and to the 26th Marines regimental headquarters in the valley to the north. All of this was beaten off without too much difficulty. The NVA's heavier columns coming down the valley

PFC Robert H. Jenkins —posthumous recipient of the Medal of Honor for gallantry while serving as a machine gunner south of the DMZ in March 1969.

of the Tuy Loan were thrown back by the 7th Marines.

As the new lunar year began, 86 percent of I Corps' populated area and 74 percent of people were optimistically considered under government control. The objective for 1969 was 100 and 90 percent, respectively. One of South Vietnam's new pacification programs was the People's Self Defense Force, or PSDF. The goal was to enroll 300,000 citizens of I Corps in the PSDF.

III MAF's most successful assist to pacification continued to be the Combined Action or 'CAP' Program. Since its beginnings at Phu Bai in 1965, it had grown to regimental size: four Combined Action groups with headquarters at Da Nang, Chu Lai, Phu Bai, and Quang Tri. These groups controlled 19 Combined Action companies which in turn controlled 102 Combined Action platoons.

PFC Oscar P. Austin —received the Medal of Honor posthumously for gallantry as an assistant machine gunner near Da Nang in February 1969.

In March, Herman Nickerson, now a lieutenant general, returned to take command of III MAF from Cushman. Nickerson had commanded the 1st Marine Division during his previous tour. The command post of that division was still on Hill 327 outside Da Nang, where he had moved it in 1966.

North of Da Nang, the first three months of 1969 had been relatively quiet for the 3d Marine Division. That division's front was a twisting, wavering turned-over 'L,' the long side being the line of the DMZ and the short side the Laotian border.

The first stirrings of renewed NVA action in the north came in April with the re-entry of the NVA 308th Division. The 9th Marines met elements of the NVA 36th Regiment between Cam Lo and the Rockpile and at the month's end the fight was formalized as Operation Virginia Ridge.

1st Lt. Wesley Lee Fox— received the Medal of Honor for gallantry while serving as commanding officer of his company at A Shau valley in February 1969. Later promoted to colonel.

Base Area 611 in Da Krong valley was refilling with NVA men and supplies and the 9th Marines went back into the valley in a replay of Dewey Canyon, this time called 'Apache Snow.' At the end of the month the 9th Marines swung north against the NVA 304th Division in the old Khe Sanh salient south of Route 9.

In mid-June the 1st Battalion, 9th Marines, joined elements of the Army's 1st Brigade, 5th Mechanized Division, for Operation Utah Mesa, near Khe Sanh. It would be the 9th Marines' last battle.

President Nixon's secret plan for ending the war

HOSEDOWN:
A machine gun team 'hoses down' an already shell-battered house near An Hoa.

was 'Vietnamization,' turning the war over to the South Vietnamese as quickly as possible. In an odd way it would make good Westmoreland's prophecy of late 1967 that Americans could be out of Vietnam in two years.

The 3d Marine Division, now commanded by Major General William K. 'Willie K' Jones, was standing down for its return to Okinawa. Twenty-five

thousand Americans were to be out of Vietnam by
31 August; 8,388 were to be Marines.

First to leave would be the 9th Marines, with cor-
responding slices of Division troops. The 1st Marine
Aircraft Wing's share would be VMFA-334, with its
F-4s, and HMM-165, with its CH-46As, along with the
1st LAAM Battalion, the air defense outfit that had
arrived in early 1965 and never had a target for its

Maj. Gen. Ormond R. Simpson —took over command of the 1st Marine Division just as the Vietnamization program began.

Hawk missiles. The Wing, now commanded by Major General William G. Thrash, had six aircraft groups with 26 squadrons flying from five major airfields.

Provisional MAG-39, chiefly helicopters, was at Quang Tri. MAG-36, all helicopters, was at Phu Bai. MAG-16, also chiefly helicopters, was at Marble Mountain. MAG-11, with mostly F-4 Phantoms and A-6A Intruders, was at Da Nang. MAG-12, with A-4 Skyhawks and A-6As, and MAG-13, with F-4s, were at Chu Lai. Two-seater AH-1G Bell Cobras had begun arriving in April. With their 7.62mm miniguns and 40mm grenade launchers, these were true gunships and they soon proved their worth. Altogether the Wing had about 225 helicopters and 250 fixed-wing aircraft—larger than most of the air forces of the world.

In Quang Nam the 1st Marine Division continued its 'paddy war.' The 26th Marines, west of Da Nang, and the 1st Marines, south of the airfield, were engaged mainly in saturation patrolling of the Rocket Belt, an arc swung around Da Nang at the extreme range of the menacing 122mm and 140mm rockets. The Rocket Belt had benefited from the installation of sensors once intended for the McNamara Wall. The 5th Marines, with its command post on Hill 55, operated chiefly to the southwest, concerned with the approaches from that direction toward Da Nang. The 5th Marines, south of the Vu Gia and Thu Bon rivers, was operating from its longtime base at An Hoa.

The completion on 30 March of the 825-foot Liberty Bridge by the Sea Bees over the Thu Bon just south of Dai Loc on the road that led to An Hoa was heralded as evidence of increasing stabilization. That same day the 5th Marines went up on Charlie Ridge in pursuit of three NVA regiments. The ARVN 51st Regiment attacked the ridge from the Thuong Duc corridor. Operation Oklahoma Hills ended with claims of 596 enemy dead and five prisoners, against Marine losses of 53 killed and 350 wounded.

Meanwhile, just to the south, the 5th Marines on 9 May intercepted a sizable NVA force coming across the much-disputed 'Arizona Territory.' After three days' fighting and with much pounding by Marine air, the intruders reeled back with a claimed loss

of 233 dead. But another NVA attack force, also pointed at Da Nang, materialized north along another familiar approach, the corridor between the highway and the railroad. In a two-day battle the 1st Marines with substantial ARVN help killed 292 of them.

The NVA offensive, uncoordinated and piecemeal, continued. On 7 June the 5th Marines encountered the newly-arrived NVA 90th Regiment in the Arizona Territory and in the next 11 days added 320 more enemy dead.

The 1st Marine Division, now commanded by Major General Ormond Simpson, began Operation Pipestone Canyon on 26 May on Go Noi island and in the 'Dodge City' area to its north to get rid of the NVA 36th Regiment once and for all. Four Marine battalions were used with two battalions of the

LIMBERING UP:
A self-propelled 175mm gun 'limbers up' for a move. In theory it could travel 375 miles at up to 35 mph. In practice, conditions were seldom suitable and guns tended to stay emplaced.

ARVN 51st Regiment, the 37th and 39th Rangers, and a battalion from the Korean Marine Brigade. They boxed in the area, and the 'clearing' operation that followed was literal: virtually every vestige of vegetation was scraped away by Marine and Army engineers using giant Rome plows.

The infestation of Viet Cong and North Vietnamese in the incredibly beautiful Que Son mountains, the natural barrier between Quang Nam and Quang Tin provinces, was unsolved.

From the air all appeared serenely bright green and sparkling silver. On foot, the mountains were

Standing Down

SO THIS IS CHRISTMAS: 25 December 1969. The oppressive tropical heat of Vietnam coupled with their heavy loads sapped even the fittest Marines. This squad from Company L, 3d Battalion, 26th Marines, takes a cooling breather in a stream after five hours humping back to Hill 190, northwest of Da Nang.

a maze of deep-cut jungled ravines and tumbling mountain streams in which the enemy could hide and sally forth at will into the lowlands.

The second increment of the US troop withdrawal was announced on 16 September. Of the 35,000 Americans to be redeployed, 18,483 would be Marines. The 3d Marines left for Camp Pendleton and the 4th Marines returned to Okinawa. General Jones shifted his flag and 3d Marine Division headquarters to Okinawa. For its 40 months in Vietnam the Division could claim 28,216 enemy killed, 499 prisoners captured, and 9,626 weapons

121

Keeping covered—a sergeant deftly converts his helmet into part of the landscape. Camouflage to the Marines was a life-saving art.

taken. A rear headquarters of the 1st Marine Aircraft Wing was activated at Iwakuni, Japan, to pick up MAG-36 and squadrons of deactivated MAG-39. One helicopter group, MAG-16, was left in I Corps. A squadron of A-6As also departed but for a time the rest of the fixed-wing squadrons would stay.

As the Marines departed, enemy action dropped back for the most part to terrorism and guerrilla activity on the Viet Cong pattern. No longer did the NVA columns come marching out of the mountains. It was as though Hanoi was glad to see the Marines go. Such contact as there was with main force units continued to be in the Que Sons and Antenna Valley, the territory of the 7th Marines. But as American strength went down, the enemy order of battle seemed to grow. The year had begun with 89 battalions listed for I Corps and it ended with 97.

The NVA brought in the New Year with an attack by its 409th Sapper Battalion against FSB Ross, held by 1st Battalion, 7th Marines. Thirty-eight of the sappers were killed and three captured but the Marines lost 13 killed and 40 wounded seriously enough to be evacuated.

The 1st Marine Division had augmented the Combined Action Program in November with something called the Infantry Company Intensive Pacification Program, which yielded the unpronounceable acronym 'ICIPP.' It began with Company M, 1st Marines, sending off rifle squads from Hill 55 into three perennially troublesome hamlets to be paired off, CAP fashion, with the local PF and RF detachments.

With the New Year, ICIPP was redesignated the Combined Unit Pacification Program, which gave the much more manageable acronym 'CUPP.' Altogether 26 squads, roughly two-thirds of a battalion, were invested in the program.

The Combined Action Program had grown during the year by the addition of another company headquarters and 13 new platoons to a total of 1,710 Marines and 119 Navy hospital corpsmen. In January the four Combined Action Groups were put under a regimental-type headquarters with the designation Combined Action Force.

By now pacification results, measured by the intricate formula known as the Hamlet Evaluation System, showed 86 percent of the over 3 million persons in I Corps to be living in secure areas, eight percent in contested areas, two percent in Viet Cong-controlled areas, and four percent unrated. On paper the war was virtually won.

The third increment of the US withdrawal, announced by Nixon in December, began in January. The Marines' share was 12,900—the core of which was the 26th Marines—to be out by 15 April 1970. It took with it most of the tracked vehicles in the Division. Four fixed-wing and one helicopter squadron also departed, leaving the 1st Marine Aircraft Wing with three groups: MAG-11 at Da Nang with four fixed-wing squadrons, MAG-13 at Chu Lai with four fixed-wing squadrons, and MAG-16 at Marble Mountain with seven squadrons of helicopters.

The Army was now the dominant US service in terms of numbers in I Corps and on 9 March, simultaneously with the detachment of General Nickerson as CG, III MAF, the respective positions of XXIV Corps and III MAF were reversed with XXIV becoming the senior command. Lieutenant General Melvin Zais, USA, moved his corps headquarters from Phu Bai down to the III MAF compound in Da Nang. The new CG, III MAF, Lieutenant General Keith McCutcheon, who had commanded the 1st Marine Aircraft Wing in the early days of the war, shifted his headquarters to Red Beach.

The area of operations for III MAF, once all of I Corps, was pared down to Quang Nam province with a thin slice of Thua Thien to the north so as to include all of Hai Van pass and a larger piece of Quang Tin, the southern boundary being the Ly Ly river in Que Son valley.

The 1st Marine Division's overriding mission continued to be protection for the populated area. The Division, now commanded by Major General Edward Wheeler, who as a colonel had brought the 3d Marines into I Corps in 1965, was disposed in a series of concentric circles. Close in to Da Nang were the Northern and Southern Sector Defense Commands, their outer edge running roughly from Marble Mountain clockwise along the Song Cau Do to include the much fought-over bridges, then along Division ridge, and on around past Nam O bridge, tying in at Red Beach. One battalion was held in

Keeping cool —a Marine turns his helmet into a portable shower to cool off in the noonday sun.

Standing Down

MOVING OUT:
A convoy of
amtracs gets
ready to move
Company D,
1st Battalion,
7th Marines
into Arizona
Territory, the
Marine
nickname for
the much-
contested
corridor south
of Da Nang.

**Staff Sgt. Alan
Jay Kellogg, Jr.
—Received the
Medal of Honor
for gallantry at
Quang Nam in
March 1970**

the Southern Sector in Division reserve and was much used in what were called 'Pacifier' operations—quick-response helicopter operations of platoon or company size after targets of opportunity.

The next ring outside the Defense Sectors was the Rocket Belt. With the departure of the 26th Marines, the 1st Marines had responsibility for the whole belt, shifting its command post from Hill 55 (taken over by the headquarters of the ARVN 51st Regiment) and moving to the area vacated by the 26th Marines close to the Division CP.

South of the 1st Marines, the Korean Marine

Brigade pursued its virtually autonomous operations west of Hoi An. Further south, beyond the Ba Ren bridge, the 7th Marines continued to work in the Que Sons and Que Son valley. To their northwest the 5th Marines continued to cover the Arizona Territory and the Thuong Duc corridor from their base at An Hoa.

General Wheeler broke his leg in a helicopter accident on 18 March and Major General Charles Widdecke took over the Division. Widdecke, with a reputation for cold efficiency, had a Navy Cross from Guam and in 1965 had brought the 5th Marines

Maj. Gen. Edwin B. Wheeler —a broken leg in a helicopter accident terminated his command.

Maj. Gen. Charles F. Widdecke —took over 1st Marine Division.

into Vietnam in 1965. President Nixon announced in April that 150,000 more Americans would be out of South Vietnam by 1 May 1971. The Marine Corps share was 41,800.

The original plan was to take out 18,600 Marines by 15 October, another 10,600 by 1 January, and the remaining 12,600, to be formed into a Marine air-ground brigade, to be out by the deadline of 1 May.

President Thieu proclaimed that henceforth the Corps Tactical Zones would be known as Military Regions, the RF and PF would become part of the Army of Vietnam, and the Civil Irregular Defense Groups would be reorganized into Ranger Border Defense Battalions. This was supposed to indicate that 'Vietnamization' was working.

General Lam, with a realistic appreciation of the dependence of his troops on the Americans, recommended that before more US troops left there be a general westward push on a broad front in what was now Military Region I.

The next principal ground unit to leave was the 7th Marines after one more crack at the Que Sons. Their last operation, Imperial Lake, was envisaged as an amphibious operation going after an island target. D-Day was 31 August and it was preceded by an all-night artillery bombardment in which 13,000 shells were fired. At 0700 the air attack began and in the next two-and-a-half hours 77 tons of ordnance, mostly 1,000-pound bombs and napalm, was dropped. The 1st Battalion then landed in the mountains. But it was no final solution, the enemy continued to be as elusive as quicksilver.

The standdown of the 7th Marines began on 7 September. The 5th Marines moved into their vacated sector, leaving An Hoa to be filled by elements of the ARVN 51st Regiment. En route to the Que Sons, the 5th Marines ran Catawba Falls, a heavy artillery and air attack aimed at the NVA 38th Regiment west of Nong Song and of the same intensity as Imperial Lake, but not followed by an infantry assault.

The 1st Marines, now commanded by Colonel Paul X. Kelley, who had commanded a battalion in 1966 and who would become a Commandant of the Marine Corps, had to stretch forward of the Rocket Belt to take over responsibility for Charlie Ridge and Thuong Duc corridor, picking up the three CUPP

MACHINE GUNNER:
The Marines at war had their own style. The first arrivals at Da Nang in 1965 stepped ashore in uniforms little changed since World War II.

But by 1968 the Marines had new jungle utilities more suited to the torpid heat of Vietnam, where midday temperatures could reach 110°. Ammunition belts worn bandolier fashion by this M-60 machine gunner and his buddy were standard fashion. The belts were loaded one in five with tracer bullets. The .45 pistol on his hip was standard issue for a machine gunner. The M-60 weighed 23 lbs. and the tripod added another 20 lbs.

positions west of Dai Loc. The parade of squadrons leaving continued. Chu Lai, with no more Marine squadrons, was turned over to the Army in October. Still operational was MAG-16 at Marble Mountain, with about 150 helicopters, and MAG-11 at Da Nang, with about 80 fixed-wing aircraft. Major General Alan J. Armstrong had replaced General Thrash as Wing commander on 1 July.

There were few close air support missions to be performed for the 1st Marine Division. The Marine F-4s continued to fly combat air patrols over Laos and the Tonkin Gulf. The A-6As, because of their all-weather capability, were much used against movers' on the Ho Chi Minh trail in Laos. The F-4s and A-4s were used to interdict such choke points in Laos as passes at Mu Gia, Ban Karai, and Ban Raving. The Combined Action Program was also

shrinking. By 1 September three of the Combined Action Groups had been deactivated and the program was down to the 2d Combined Action Group in Quang Nam with six companies and 38 platoons.

Then the redeployment plan was changed. Now 17,021 Marines were to depart by 15 October instead of 18,600. The increment that was to leave by 1 January was postponed until 30 April. There was no firm decision as to how long the brigade made up of the remainder would stay.

Standing Down

CHARLIE RIDGE:
Marines of the 1st Battalion, 7th Marines engage the enemy on Charlie Ridge in February 1970.
The standing Marine is using an M-16, apparently at full automatic. The kneeling Marine is armed with the heavier M-14 with a bipod in full-automatic mode.

The overstretched 51st Regiment was slow in taking over An Hoa. Only enough ARVN soldiers could be spared to man a quarter of the sprawling base. The move was also hampered by the monsoon rains that began in October. Typhoon Kate caused the worst floods since 1964 and for a time III MAF did more flood relief than fighting.

The 195th birthday of the Corps was celebrated on 10 November with a great cake-cutting ceremony in a hangar at the Da Nang air base. Veteran screen star Martha Raye, a favorite of the III MAF Marines, was guest of honor and General McCutcheon presided. He had been nominated by President Nixon for a fourth star and was to succeed General Walt as Assistant Commandant on 1 February. By now, though, it was obvious that he was not well. On 11 December he returned to his headquarters from the hospital ship *Sanctuary,* where some tests had been made, and told his general officers that he was leaving in two days for hospitalization at Bethesda. He had terminal cancer.

Donn J. Robertson, who had commanded the 1st Marine Division in 1968 and 1969, was quickly promoted to lieutenant general and flown to Da Nang. He presided over the final phase-out of the much truncated III Marine Amphibious Force.

William K. Jones, now a lieutenant general and Commanding General, Fleet Marine Force, Pacific, discussed with Robertson what came next in III MAF's redeployments. In the next increment, 11,207 Marines would be redeployed before 30 April. The remaining 13,604 would be organized into the 3d Marine Amphibious Brigade under General Armstrong.

American units no longer had "tactical areas of *responsibility*"; they had "tactical areas of *interest*." This fine point of doctrinal change which appeared in the Combined Campaign Plan for 1971 was probably lost on the Marine rifleman picking his dangerous way through the paddies and hamlets south of Da Nang, but it meant, in theory, that the 1st Marine Division no longer had primary responsibility for the security of Quang Nam.

Entertainer Martha Raye —cutting the cake as guest of honor at the Marines' 195th birthday party at Da Nang

Westmoreland's long-cherished plan for a move westward from Route 9 into Laos was about to take place, but III MAF subordinate commanders knew nothing until 30 January, when they were briefed on the essentials by XXIV Corps staff. Lam Son 719 was to be an ARVN spoiling attack to knock off balance what appeared to be an enemy build-up for a major offensive into Military Region I. The North Vietnamese were thought to have 24,000 troops, 11 regiments.

The operation was to be in four phases.

Phase I, to last five days, was the opening of Route 9 by the 1st Brigade, 5th Mechanized Brigade, from Vandegrift west to abandoned Khe Sanh. Phase II would be the helicopter movement of ARVN I Corps west along the axis of Route 9, cutting across the Ho Chi Minh trail complex as far as the ruined town of Tchepone 40 kilometers into Laos.

Phase III would be a systematic search-and-destroy operation in Base Area 604 believed to be in the vicinity of Tchepone.

Phase IV would be the withdrawal, coming out south of Route 9 through Base Area 611.

General Lam had gone out along Route 9 with the French against the Viet Minh as a young lieutenant. He often talked about it. For this foray he had the well-regarded ARVN 1st Division, the 1st Armored Brigade, and his Ranger Group, and from the JGS strategic reserve sizable numbers of Airborne troops and Vietnamese Marines.

Lt. Gen. Donn J. Robertson —hurriedly promoted to preside over the final phase-out of III Marine Amphibious Force.

US Marine Corps involvement was to be small. The 1st Marine Division was to provide extra security for Highway One, particularly in Hai Van pass. A company of 5-ton trucks and some engineer equipment was to be sent north. The 1st Marine Aircraft Wing was to provide some heavy-helilift with its CH-54s, and, through the Seventh Air Force, fixed-wing tactical air support.

On 8 February, slightly behind schedule, Lam's forces crossed into Laos. Marine heavy helicopters lifted a million pounds of cargo into Khe Sanh. Camp Carroll was also reopened. At first there was almost no opposition, but it built up until three NVA divisions, four artillery regiments, and a tank regiment were identified.

No American ground troops, not even advisors, were allowed to accompany Lam's corps. The absence of American advisors was particularly damaging because of the absence of their liaison and communications. The lingering 'crachin,' with its morning drizzle and fog, interfered with air support. US Marine participation continued to be limited to tactical air and daily 'packages' of CH-53s escorted by Cobras.

The ARVN fire support bases, set up to the American formula, turned into bull's eyes for the profusion of hidden North Vietnamese artillery. By the end of February, Tchepone was reached and found empty. Lam's staff had proved too thin to conduct such an ambitious operation. There was dissension between his troops and the Airborne and

Marine units provided by Saigon. Lam, his corps in
disarray and on the edge of disaster, salvaged the
situation by reporting the objectives accomplished.
The pull-out began.

The South Vietnamese admitted to 1,483 ARVN
killed, 5,420 wounded, and 691 missing. Material
losses, particularly in heavy equipment and
weapons, were horrendous. American casualties,
mostly US Army, were 176 killed, 1,048 wounded,
and 42 missing. In February, Marine CH-53s had
lifted 968 passengers and 4,436 tons of cargo in support of the operation and the Wing's attack aircraft

had dropped 1,183 tons of ordnance. In March, on the way out, the heavy helicopters lifted 1,556 troops and 1,491 tons of cargo. Only one Marine heavy helicopter was lost but US Army helicopter losses were heavy. President Thieu held a victory parade in Hue. The Americans wondered why.

The departure of III MAF Marines continued while Lam Son 719 was being fought. On 15 February, the 3d Battalion, 5th Marines, stood down, moving from FSB Ross to Hill 34 south of Da Nang. The 3d Battalion was followed by the 2d Battalion and the regimental headquarters from LZ Baldy. The 1st

GOING HOME:
Helicopters streaming smoke do a fly-by in salute of the 1st Marine Division as it began its re-deployment home in March 1971.

Marines put a battalion into the Que Sons to continue Imperial Lake and to cover Baldy until the Vietnamese were ready to take it over.

Colonel Kelley's 1st Marines continued to work the Rocket Belt. There was a standing reward of a recreation leave to Hong Kong or Bangkok for any Marine who found a rocket. No rockets impacted in January, 21 arrived in February, and 36 in March, reflecting, perhaps, the thinning of the Marine ranks.

VMFA-115, the last Marine F-4 squadron at Da Nang, flew its last mission on 22 February and then left for Iwakuni. Medium helicopter squadron HMM-364 departed for Santa Ana on 11 March. Observation squadron VMO-2 left for Camp Pendleton on 8 April.

On 29 March the enemy dropped 23 rockets on Da Nang air base and it surroundings. That same night there were attacks against the district headquarters at Dien Ban, Dai Loc, Que Son, and Duc Duc. The message was clear: "The Americans are leaving, but *we* are still here."

The 1st Marines, responding to a not-really-believed intelligence report from MACV that there was a Viet Cong POW camp in the west of Quang Nam, made one last foray, Operation Scott Orchard,

PARTING SHOT: Da Nang air base was never safe from Viet Cong rocket attacks. Here an American airplane goes up in flames. Less than two months before the Marines stood down the enemy dropped 23 rockets on Da Nang. The message was clear: 'The Americans are leaving but *we* are still here.'

beginning 7 April. FSB Dagger was reopened and five companies under 2d Battalion, 1st Marines, prowled the jungle for a last time. No POW camp or POWs were found, four enemy were killed, and 12 weapons taken. The US Army's 196th Light Infantry Brigade moved into the Que Sons on 13 April. Everything south of the Vu Gia-Thu Bon rivers was now, using the new terminology, no longer 'of interest' to the Marines. In a quixotic gesture the location of Imperial Lake was shifted to Charlie Ridge.

On 14 April, in a solemn ceremony at Red Beach, the colors of the III Marine Amphibious Force, of the 1st Marine Division, and of the 1st Marine Aircraft Wing snapped in the breeze coming off the China Sea for a last time and were cased.

The operational life of 3d MAB was short. On 7 April President Nixon had announced that the 3d MAB was to be out by 1 July. The 1st Battalion, 1st Marines, had already stood down. It was soon followed by the 3d Battalion.

All ground and air combat ended for 3d MAB on 7 May. The last 18 CAP platoons were deactivated. Hamlet and village security had begun to crumble. The 2d Battalion, 1st Marines, the last Marine infantry battalion in the field, was south of the Song Cau Do. General Raymond Davis, now the Assistant Commandant of the Marine Corps, had lunch with Company F on the sand flats. The closest village was Cam Ne, from which Morley Safer had made his famous broadcast in 1965.

By 26 May, the last day of Marine helicopter operations, the 2d Battalion, 1st Marines, was on its way to Camp Pendleton. On 1 June the US Army took over Marble Mountain Air Facility.

Left behind in all of South Vietnam were something like 500 Marines in what Washington's redeployment plans called "transitional-support." Some were guards at the US Embassy in Saigon and the US Consulate in Da Nang. There was still a Marine advisory unit of about 60 officers and men with the Vietnamese Marine Corps, which had grown to a three-brigade division. The largest number, though, were in the 1st Air and Naval Gunfire Liaison Company. More familiarly known as 'ANGLICO,' these Marines were parceled out in teams from the DMZ down to the southern tip of the country. Their time was coming.

US President Richard M. Nixon
—his "secret" plan to end the war was Vietnamization accompanied by phased withdrawal of US forces, and the threat of increased bombing of North Vietnam.

Easter Offensive

Attacks Across the DMZ

THE PATTERN of the North Vietnamese Easter 1972 offensive was not new, but its weight was.

In the north, one NVA division crossed the DMZ into Quang Tri, while another moved east along Route 9. A third NVA division marched into Thua Thien through A Shau valley toward Hue. In the south, three NVA divisions advanced out of Cambodia along the axis of Route 13. In the center, the third prong emerged more slowly, two divisions coming out of Laos along the old invasion route through the Central Highlands, first to Dak To and then toward Kontum.

In Quang Tri the converging divisions were supported by at least 200 tanks and large numbers of 122mm and 130mm Soviet-model field guns. Big surface-to-air missiles—the dreaded 'SAMs'—had been moved south, almost to the DMZ, to ward off tactical air support. There were plentiful 12.7mm to 57mm anti-aircraft guns in the advancing columns. The SA-7, a Russian-made heat-seeking missile similar to the US Redeye, was also reported.

The new ARVN 3d Division failed to hold this weight of advance and the old combat bases—Khe Sanh, Camp Carroll, Con Thien, Gio Linh—were rolled up one after the other.

The 258th Brigade took a pounding at Dong Ha but held all positions. Its 3d Battalion was defending the bridge over the Cua Viet at Dong Ha. On 2 April, as the enemy's armored column reached the far side, Captain John W. Ripley, battalion's advisor, made five trips out onto the fireswept bridge, emplaced 500 pounds of explosive, and blew up the bridge in one of the most spectacular feats of bravery of the war. He received the Navy Cross.

Brigade 258 then withdrew toward Quang Tri

MARINES

Easter Offensive

BACK IN: No Marine ground combat units were re-introduced into South Vietnam to counter N.Vietnam's 1972 Easter Offensive.

But the Marines did provide substantial aviation and logistical help for the beleaguered South Vietnamese. Here on 24 May, Lt. Col. James A. Poland, adviser to the South Vietnamese Marines, brings in a flight of CH-46s from Marine Medium Helicopter Squadron 164 (HMM-164) to a landing strip near Hue.

City. The next day, the Joint General Staff ordered Lieutenant General Nguyen Le Khang to take his Vietnamese Marine Division headquarters and his last brigade, 369, north. Khang set up his command post in the Citadel in Hue. His senior advisor was Colonel Joshua W. Dorsey III, who in 1965 and 1966 had commanded a battalion in the 3d Marines. Brigade 369 went into action near FSB Nancy. Brigade 147, badly in need of refitting, was pulled

back to Hue. Meanwhile, the 9th Marine Amphibious Brigade, commanded by Brigadier General Edward J. Miller and with four battalion landing teams and two composite helicopter squadrons, was standing off the mouth of the Cua Viet. Miller was forbidden to land any ground combat troops; his support was to be limited to amphibian tractors and helicopters.

The Seventh Fleet had every available cruiser and

McDonnell Douglas F-4B and F-4J Phantom II —This was the standard Marine fighter/attack aircraft of the Vietnam War. Each Marine fighter/attack squadron (VMFA) had a complement of 15 aircraft. A typical bomb load in Vietnam would be twelve 500-lb. iron bombs.

destroyer on the gun line off South Vietnam's coast, ready to respond to demands for fire from the ANGLICO teams. Most requests came from Military Region 1.

Colonel Keith O'Keefe's MAG-15 with two F-4J squadrons, VMFAs 115 and 232, arrived at Da Nang. A third Phantom squadron, VMFA-212, arrived from Hawaii. O'Keefe's group provided tactical support to Military Region 1 and Military Region 2, where the North Vietnamese column, if it were not stopped in the Central Highlands, might cut the country in two.

The battered ARVN 3d Division formed a rough line along the south bank of the Cua Viet. Khang sent the now rested Brigade 147 north again to relieve Brigade 258 on that line. The Cua Viet line, however, crumbled under a North Vietnamese attack on 27 April. Three days later Brigade 147 became the rearguard for the 3d Division as it withdrew in disorder from Quang Tri City. Two days later the city fell.

Brigade 369 made the next attempt at a defensive line along the My Chanh river, the boundary between Quang Tri and Thua Thien provinces. Brigade 258 moved into this line west of Brigade 369. The 147th Brigade fell back to regroup, once again, in Hue.

By 4 May all of Quang Tri province was lost to the North Vietnamese. The ARVN 3d Division, by now completely ineffective, continued to retire south along Highway One to Quang Nam province, into camps once occupied by the 1st Marine Division.

Khang was given operational control of the 1st Ranger Group and the 2d Airborne Brigade and his own three brigades. These five brigades were all that stood between the North Vietnamese and Hue and Da Nang. The North Vietnamese, after regrouping, resumed the offensive in mid-May, driving south toward Hue. The My Chanh line held them off north of the city while the veteran ARVN 1st Division defended the western approaches. Khang now undertook a limited amphibious envelopment, landing Brigade 147 16 kilometers south of Quang Tri City, then sweeping south between Highway One and the sea, all backed up by vast amounts of US naval gunfire and air support.

MAG-12, under Colonel Dean C. Macho, arrived

in mid-May at Bien Hoa air base in Military Region 3, with two squadrons of A-4 Skyhawks, which concentrated strikes in the south and along the border with Cambodia.

Task Force Delta was reactivated under 1st Marine Aircraft Wing's assistant wing commander Brigadier General Andrew W. O'Donnell, to open up the never-completed air base at Nam Phong in Thailand, about 300 miles from Da Nang and Hanoi. A Marine recruiting campaign was pegged to the slogan: "We don't promise you a rose garden," and Nam Phong promptly became the 'Rose Garden.'

VMFA-115 with its F-4s shifted to the Rose Garden from Da Nang and began operations from its 10,000-foot concrete strip. On the 20th, MAG-15 headquarters and VMFA-232, the 'Red Devils,' came over from Da Nang. Within a week, VMA(AW)-533 with its A-6A Intruders was also present.

The full Airborne Division had now joined Khang's Marine Division north of Hue. On 28 June these two crack divisions counterattacked, the Airborne troopers on the left and the Marines on the right, next to the sea. The shoulder-to-shoulder advance along the axis of Highway One went well until the North Vietnamese defense of Quang Tri City was met.

The invaders were determined to hold the city and its Citadel, the battle becoming a prolonged re-play of the battle for Hue of four years before. The North Vietnamese defense was centered on the 50-acre Citadel, with its 15-foot stone walls. The South Vietnamese twice prematurely announced its recapture and on 27 July the JGS withdrew the Airborne Division, leaving Khang's Marine Division to finish the fight.

On another too-familiar battlefield, Que Son valley, a fresh North Vietnamese column drove the ARVN 5th Regiment, 2d Division, out of FSB Ross and Que Son district headquarters. These positions were eventually retaken but the 2d Division's control of the Que Son mountains and valley was only tenuous.

In early September, Khang's Marines prepared a final assault against Quang Tri's Citadel. Brigade 258 was on the Division's left front and Brigade 147 on the right, with the Song Vinh Dinh between them. The 1st Ranger Group relieved Brigade 147

Location of the 'Rose Garden' of Nam Phong and other principal airfields of Vietnam.

Easter Offensive

ROCKETPROOF: To counter rocket attacks at Da Nang, protective revetments were installed at US airbases. As part of US reaction to the Easter Offensive, MAG-12 and its A-4 Skyhawks returned to Bien Hoa and MAG-15 and its F-4 Phantoms returned to Da Nang. None were lost to rocket fire.

in the lines, allowing it to swing around and come in at the Citadel from the northeast. The final attack began at dawn on 9 September, with six battalions of the Vietnamese Marine Division.

Two days of bitter fighting followed. Then a platoon from the 6th Battalion, Brigade 258, broke through a hole blasted in the Citadel's south wall by US jets. The rest of the battalion stormed through the breach to take the southeast quarter of the fort.

Marble Mountain Air Facility on China Beach near Da Nang offered almost factory-like conditions for the maintenance of US Marine planes and helicopters.

Meanwhile, other Vietnamese Marines scaled the north and east walls. By nightfall on 15 September the Citadel had been cleared and next day, at noon, the yellow-and-red flag of South Vietnam was flying over the gate.

This finished the North Vietnamese Spring 1972 invasion. With Dr. Henry Kissinger in Paris talking with Le Duc Tho, it looked as though peace might be at hand.

Frequent Wind

Evacuating Cambodia and Vietnam

IN PARIS, after four years of negotiation, the 'Peace Accords' were signed on 27 January 1973 by all four sides of the round table: North and South Vietnam, the Viet Cong, and the United States. The Accords seemingly ended what had become an impossibly unpopular war for the United States without the appearance of complete abandonment of their South Vietnamese ally.

The ceasefire was to go into effect at midnight. Free general elections were promised. Until then the Saigon and Hanoi governments would remain in power. All foreign troops were to be out of South Vietnam within 60 days and their bases dismantled. The Nobel Peace Prize was offered jointly to Henry Kissinger and Le Duc Tho, the negotiators. Kissinger accepted but Tho declined, saying he would reconsider it after "real peace is established in South Vietnam."

In February and March, 591 American prisoners of war came home; 26 were Marines. Nine other Marine prisoners had escaped. Three more had been exchanged earlier. Seven others died in captivity.

The ceasefire was to be monitored by an International Commission of Control and Supervision made up of equal numbers of members from Canada, Indonesia, Hungary, and Poland. Almost immediately there were violations on both sides. In July 1973 Canada quit the Commission in frustration and was replaced by Iran.

Most of Quang Tri province was soon nibbled away by the North Vietnamese and Khe Sanh and Dong Ha became North Vietnamese bases.

This uneasy 'peace' continued for almost two years, but in mid-December 1974 the North Vietnamese marched boldly into Phuoc Long. Three

URBAN LZ:
A Marine CH-53 helicopter sets down at Ton Son Nhut airfield near Saigon ready to pick up evacuees in Operation Frequent Wind.

weeks later their flag flew over Phuoc Binh, the province capital, only 40 miles north of Saigon.

President Nguyen Van Thieu did not try to eject them. A full-scale North Vietnamese invasion followed, with three major thrusts similar to 1972.

The NVA 10th and 316th Divisions attacked the Central Highlands and on 10 March, after a week, took the Montagnard capital of Ban Me Thuot. South Vietnam's defensive arc was punctured, causing Thieu to attempt to withdraw from the Highlands and the north to concentrate around Saigon and the vital coastal areas.

Thieu's new strategy was to 'lighten the top' to 'keep the bottom.' He told his I Corps commander, Lieutenant General Ngo Quang Truong, to give up most of Military Region 1. He was to hold Da Nang. What Saigon was to the country, Da Nang was to I Corps.

Thieu ordered the II Corps to evacuate the Highlands and to shift headquarters from Pleiku to Nha Trang on the coast. The general withdrawal was too much for Thieu's sedentary divisions. The whole, broad front began to crumble. Provinces were lost at the rate of one a day.The Vietnamese Marines were shifted from position to position as the situation disintegrated. Those who were not killed or captured left Da Nang in great disorder, many jammed on Vietnamese Navy and US merchant ships that took them to Vung Tau. Da Nang fell without a fight.

In Cambodia, the Khmer Rouge were also on the offensive. By March they had encircled the capital, Phnom Penh. President Lon Nol left the city on 1 April, on the first leg of a self-imposed exile to Hawaii.

In the Gulf of Siam, the amphibious ships of the Seventh Fleet, with the 31st Marine Amphibious Unit embarked, awaited orders to execute Eagle Pull, the planned evacuation of Americans and other foreign nationals. The order came from President Gerald Ford on 12 April. In two hours two squadrons of CH-53 Sea Stallions took out 84 Americans and 203 others, including some high-ranking Cambodians.

By now the North Vietnamese were in Qui Nhon, Tuy Hoa, Nha Trang, and Cam Ranh. Ton Son Nhut, outside of Saigon, and Bien Hoa, just 15 miles to the northeast, were the only two jet-capable air bases left to the South Vietnamese. Between the North Vietnamese and Bien Hoa was Xuan Loc on Highway One determinedly defended by the ARVN 18th Division. The new Vietnamese Marine 468th Brigade joined the 18th Division at Long Binh for a last stand.

Lying off Vung Tau, the 9th Marine Amphibious

PROTECTIVE SECURITY: As the fall of Saigon approached, relationships between the S. Vietnamese and Americans reached an all-time low. On board ships carrying refugees Marines were posted to act as policemen. Marines escort South Vietnamese pilots under close security to an inspection point aboard *USS Hancock* during the evacuation.

Brigade was waiting for orders to take out the rest of the Americans. Brigadier General Richard E. Carey commanded the brigade. Now an aviator, Carey had served in Korea as a rifle and machine gun platoon leader. His brigade included Regimental Landing Team 4 (built around the 4th Marines), Provisional Marine Aircraft Group 39, and the Brigade Logistical Support Group. There was also an Amphibious Evacuation Force of security platoons formed to act as policemen on board the ships carrying tens of thousands of frantic Vietnamese refugees.

Brig.Gen. Richard E. Carey— former infantryman turned aviator who commanded the Marines during Operation Frequent Wind.

A five-man advance party from the Brigade flew into Saigon on 20 April. The party was dismayed by the Alice-in-Wonderland attitude of the American community. It was as though the inevitable had been pushed out of their consciousness.

There were supposed to be some 6,000 Americans still in the city, but no one was certain. No one could guess the number of Vietnamese who wanted to flee the city.

President Thieu resigned on 21 April. He left for Taiwan four days later after bitterly describing his "desertion" by the United States as "an inhumane act by an inhumane ally."

Vice President Tran Van Huong, 71 years old and ailing, held the presidency for a week and then turned the office over to General Duong Van Minh. The same 'Big' Minh who had taken over after the demise of Diem nearly 12 years earlier, he was ready to surrender Saigon.

In the last week large numbers of Americans, foreign nationals and Vietnamese escaped by fixed-wing transports, some US Air Force and some chartered, flying from Ton Son Nhut.

The North Vietnamese took Xuan Loc, snuffing out the last vestige of organized resistance. They paused in the outskirts of Saigon.

Before dawn on 29 April, rockets exploded at Ton Son Nhut, killing two Marine guards at the Defense Attache Office. In Washington, President Ford called the National Security Council and at 22.45 ordered the execution of Frequent Wind, the final departure of the Americans from Saigon.

General Carey received the order on board the command ship *Blue Ridge.*

Two heavy helicopter squadrons, HMH-462 and HMH-463, flying CH-53s, began bringing in what

Frequent Wind

PARKING GIANTS:
Two Marine CH-53 Sea Stallions set down in a compound near Saigon's Ton Son Nhut air base ready to evacuate American civilians and foreign nationals. The helicopters had a lift capacity of 37 passengers plus three crew. When the order was received mid-morning on 29 April 1975 to begin Operation Frequent Wind, two squadrons of CH-53s and two squadrons of CH-46 Sky Knights flew non-stop missions from Saigon to the awaiting ships. By midnight they had evacuated 4,870 civilians.

was now called the Ground *Security* Force. Some 865 members of BLT 2/4 were landed at the tennis courts once used by Westmoreland and his MACV staff. Before nightfall three platoons were sent forward by helicopter to the Embassy compound, bringing the total number of Marines there to 171.

Returning to their ships, the heavy helicopters took out 395 Americans and 4,475 Vietnamese by midnight. The last Marines to leave set fire to what once had been called 'Pentagon East.'

In Saigon, the US Embassy was besieged by a mob
of Vietnamese, would-be refugees, and street gangs
eager to loot the premises. The gates had to be locked
and late-arriving Americans were lifted over the
walls by muscular Marines. There were just two
places where helicopters could land. The roof of the
Embassy could take the medium CH-46. The heavy
CH-53s could land one at a time on the Embassy
parking lot.

Carey's information was that there were only a

Vietnamese refugees commandeered whatever craft they could to seek refuge on board US ships in the South China Sea. Here they line up to board *USS Durham*, which ferried them to another ship for passage to a safe zone.

hundred Americans to be taken out, but the evacuation went on all night and the count went up to 978 Americans (including some rather strange ones) and 1,120 foreign nationals and Vietnamese.

The North Vietnamese, now in Saigon, were preparing a triumphant May Day takeover. There was no organized resistance to the evacuation, only a good deal of harassing ground fire against the aircraft, coming, it is to be supposed, also from disgruntled South Vietnamese. There were no combat casualties, although one CH-46 along with its two pilots was lost at sea. An AH-1J Cobra ditched at sea after running out of fuel, but its pilots were rescued.

As morning approached, the Vietnamese mob battered down the gate with a firetruck. Hysterical Vietnamese poured into the Embassy compound. The Marine Security Guard backed its way up the staircases, floor by floor to the roof. The last CH-46, carrying the last 11 Marines, took off at 07.53, 30 April.

III MARINE Amphibious Force, at its peak strength in 1968, had 85,755 Marines ashore—more than a quarter of the Marine Corps' total strength and more Marines than fought at Iwo Jima or Okinq.

During the longer Vietnam War some 730,000 men and women served in the Corps, against some 600,000 in World War II. Perhaps 500,000 Marines served in Vietnam.

A Marine would serve 12 or 13 months and then return home. During the height of the war some 9,000 to 10,000 replacements arrived each month in Vietnam to keep up III MAF's strength. To feed this pipeline some 85,000 to 120,000 Marines entered and left the Marine Corps each year.

In World War II, the Marines lost 19,733 killed and 67,207 wounded. In Vietnam the figures, as of 1986, are 13,067 killed or dead as a result of enemy action, and 88,633 wounded, of whom 51,389 required hospitalization.

These figures are nearly a third of all American casualties. Of the 826 known American prisoners of war, only 47 were Marines. Another 105 Marines are still listed as missing in action—out of a total 1,156 Americans—and two others still remain unaccounted for.

Frequent Wind

GOING HOME: Throughout the war the Marine Corps tradition of never leaving its fallen behind, was extended, whenever possible, to its equipment. The principle was put into action as early as 1965. Here, a troop-carrying UH-34 helicopter has been dismantled so that a larger helicopter could airlift it out and thereby salvage a quarter-million-dollar aircraft.

A-4	— Douglas 'Skyhawk,' a single-seat, light jet attack aircraft.
A-6A	— Grumman 'Intruder,' a two-seat, twin-jet, all-weather attack aircraft.
AK-47	— Russian-designed 'Kalishnikov' gas-operated 7.62mm automatic rifle with an effective range of 400 meters.
ANGLICO	— Air and Naval Gunfire Liaison Company, an organization of Marine and Navy personnel specifically qualified to provide control of naval gunfire and close air support for units other than US Marines.
Arc Light	— The codename for B-52 bombing missions in South Vietnam.
ARVN	— Army of the Republic of Vietnam (South Vietnam). Pronounced 'arvin.'
B-52	— Boeing 'Stratofortress,' a US Air Force eight-engine, swept-wing, heavy jet bomber.
BLT	— Battalion landing team.
C-117D	— Douglas 'Skytrain,' a twin-engine transport aircraft. See also 'KC-130.'
CAP	— See 'Combined Action Program.'
CH-37	— Sikorsky 'Deuce,' a twin-engine, heavy transport helicopter.
CH-46	— Boeing Vertol 'Sea Knight,' a twin-turbine, tandem-rotor medium transport helicopter.
CH-53	— Sikorsky 'Sea Stallion,' a single-rotor, heavy transport helicopter powered by two shaft-turbine engines.
CIDG	— Civilian Irregular Defense Group, a South Vietnamese paramilitary force, made up largely of Montagnards, the tribesmen of the Central Highlands, and advised by US Special Forces.

CinCPac	— Commander in Chief, Pacific.
CinCPacFlt	— Commander in Chief, Pacific Fleet.
CMC	— Commandant of the Marine Corps.
Combined Action Program	— Marine-initiated pacification technique which integrated a Marine rifle squad with a South Vietnamese Popular Force platoon for hamlet and village security.
Com USMACV	— Commander, US Military Assistance Command, Vietnam.
County Fair	— A cordon-and-search technique, designed to root out Viet Cong infrastructure, involving South Vietnamese troops and officials and US Marines in the screening of village and hamlet inhabitants.
CP	— Command post, a unit's field headquarters.
CTZ	— Corps Tactical Zone, principal military and political territorial sub-division of the Republic of South Vietnam.
DMZ	— Demilitarized Zone along the 17th Parallel that separated North and South Vietnam. Established by the Geneva Accords of 1954.
Eagle Pull	— Code name for final US evacuation from Cambodia in 1975.
F-4B	— McDonnell 'Phantom II,' a twin-engined, two-seat, long-range jet interceptor and attack bomber.
FMFPac	— Fleet Marine Force, Pacific.
Frequent Wind	— Code name for final US evacuation from South Vietnam in 1975.
Golden Fleece	— Marine rice harvest protection operation.
HAWK	— A surface-to-air guided missile designed to defend against low-flying aircraft and short range missiles.

HEAT	— High-explosive, anti-tank.
I Corps	— The military and political subdivision which included the five northern provinces of South Vietnam.
JCS	— Joint Chiefs of Staff (United States).
JGS	— Joint General Staff (South Vietnam).
KC-130	— The in-flight refueling tanker configuration of the C-130 Lockheed 'Hercules.'
KIA	— Killed-in-action.
Kit Carson Scouts	— Viet Cong defectors recruited by Marines to serve as scouts, interpreters, and intelligence agents.
LZ	— Landing zone for helicopters.
MAB	— Marine Amphibious Brigade.
MACV	— Military Assistance Command, Vietnam. Pronounced "mac-vee", it was the senior US military headquarters in South Vietnam.
MAF	— Marine Amphibious Force.
MAG	— Marine Aircraft Group.
Main Force	— Organized Viet Cong battalions and regiments as opposed to local VC guerrilla groups or hamlet militia.
MIA	— Missing-in-action.
NVA	— North Vietnamese Army, often used colloquially to refer to a North Vietnamese soldier.
PAVN	— Peoples Army of Vietnam (North Vietnam). Usage dropped in favor of 'NVA.'
PF	— Popular Force, South Vietnamese hamlet and village militia.
RF	— Regional Force. South Vietnamese provincial militia.
RPG	— Rocket propelled grenade.
RVNAF	— Republic of Vietnam Armed Forces.

SATS	— Short Airfield for Tactical Support, an expeditionary airfield used at Chu Lai, employing a portable runway surface and aircraft launching and recovery devices.
SLF	— Special Landing Force, Seventh Fleet's embarked amphibious reserve consisting usually of a battalion landing team and a helicopter squadron.
Stingray	— Marine reconnaissance missions in which five-or-six man teams called artillery and air attacks on targets of opportunity.
TAC	— Tactical Air Command.
TAOR	— Tactical area of operational responsibility.
Tet	— Vietnamese for the lunar New Year. The enemy offensive of 1968 gave it special significance.
UH-1E	— Bell 'Huey,' a single-engine light helicopter used primarily for observation, command, and control.
UH-34D	— Sikorsky 'Sea Horse,' a single-engine medium transport helicopter.
USA	— United States Army.
USAF	— United States Air Force.
USMC	— United States Marine Corps.
USN	— United States Navy.
VC or Viet Cong	— A contraction of the Vietnamese phrase meaning 'Vietnamese Communist.'
Viet Minh	— A contraction of 'Viet Nam Doc Lap Nong Minh Hoi,' the Communist-led coalition that opposed the French in the First Indo-China War, 1947-1954.
VNAF	— Vietnamese Air Force.
VNMC	— Vietnamese Marine Corps.
VNN	— Vietnamese Navy.
WIA	— Wounded-in-action.

About the Author

General Simmons

The author, Brigadier General Edwin H. Simmons, had two tours of duty in Vietnam. From July 1965 until July 1966 he served as G-3 or operations officer of III Marine Amphibious Force before being named Commanding Officer of the 9th Marine Regiment.

In 1968 he returned for another one-year tour and served as Assistant Division Commander with the 1st Marine Division and subsequently as Deputy Commander, 3d Marine Amphibious Brigade.

The author of numerous books and articles on military history, his best-known work is his history, *The United States Marine Corps, 1775-1975.*

He is currently the Director of Marine Corps History and Museums, a position he has held since 1971. He is also a past President of the American Military Institute and Executive Vice-President of the Marine Corps Historical Foundation.

Born in Paulsboro, New Jersey, in 1921, he joined the Marine Corps in 1942 after graduating from Lehigh University. During his active duty years he served in combat in World War II and the Korean War as well as the Vietnam War and has commanded every level of unit from platoon to division.

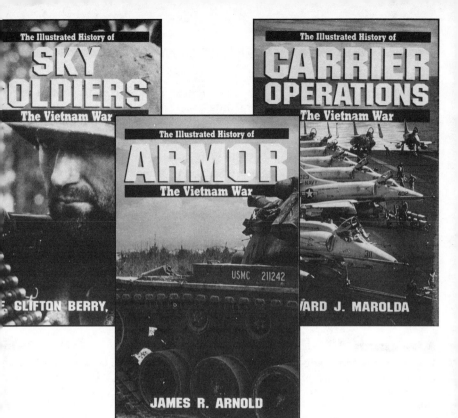

THE ILLUSTRATED
HISTORY OF
THE VIETNAM WAR

antam's Illustrated History of the
ietnam War is a unique and new
eries of books exploring in depth the
ar that seared America to the core:
war that cost 58,022 American lives,
hat saw great heroism and re-
ourcefulness mixed with terrible
estruction and tragedy.

The Illustrated History of the Viet-
am War examines exactly what hap-
ened: every significant aspect—the
hysical details, the operations and
the strategies behind them—is ana-
lyzed in short, crisply written original
books by established historians and
journalists.

Some books are devoted to key battles and campaigns, others unfold the
stories of elite groups and fighting
units, while others focus on the role
of specific weapons and tactics.

Each volume is totally original and
is richly illustrated with photographs,
line drawings, and maps.

AVAILABLE NOW

Sky Soldiers
F.Clifton Berry, Jr.

The 173d Airborne was the first major American ground combat unit to launch offensive operations in a major parachute attack. And they were the last out. This is their story.
$6.95/$8.95 in Canada ISBN:0-553-34320-3

Armor
James R. Arnold

At the start of the war it was wrongly believed that armor would be useless in Vietnam. But the Pentagon strategists were wrong. Armor was able to move quickly and produce devastating firepower against an elusive enemy constantly on the move.
$6.95/$8.95 in Canada ISBN:0-553-34347-5

Carrier Operations
Edward J. Marolda

Yankee and Dixie Stations...just two map coordinates in the South China Sea. But for the duration of the Vietnam War they were home to thousands of sailors on board the aircraft carriers of the US Seventh Fleet. It was from these offshore oases that US aircraft waged the heaviest bombing campaign in history.
$6.95/$8.95 in Canada ISBN:0-553-34348-

OCTOBER 1987

Khe Sanh
Mike Ewing

For 77 days without adequate supplies of water or ammo 6,000 isolated Marines defended the remote rust-red plateau of Khe Sanh. In the White House an anxious president declared that Khe Sanh must not fall. This account tells how close the US came to losing one of the most controversial actions of the war
$6.95/$8.95 in Canada ISBN:0-553-34458-

Tunnel Warfare
Tom Mangold & John Penycate

The secret network of tunnels around Saigon was the battleground for the most harrowing campaign of the war. This was combat at its most claustrophobic. Armed with often nothing more than knives, pistols, and flashlights, US volunteers, known as "Tunnel Rats," took on Viet Cong guerillas, who had lived for years below ground. On both sides there were heroes and moments of incredible courage. This account does justice to the men who fought underground.
$6.95/$8.95 in Canada ISBN:0-553-34318

DECEMBER 1987

Artillery
James R. Arnold

Firepower superiority was critical to the US war effort. The solution was a system of linked hilltop Fire Support Bases—a unique development in the use of artillery
$6.95/$8.95 in Canada ISBN:0-553-34319

Riverine Force
Victor Croizat

The compelling story of the hastily-assembled brown water navy faced with the nightmare task of securing South Vietnam's 3,500-mile labyrinth of waterways
$6.95/$8.95 in Canada ISBN:0-553-34317

**Available at your local bookstore or call Bantam Books direct at
1-800-223-6834. (In New York State call 212-765-6500 ext.479.)**